The Invisible Boy

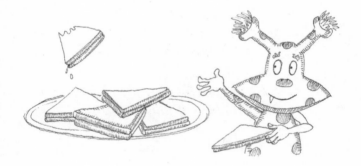

ALSO BY SALLY GARDNER

The Magical Children series

The Boy Who Could Fly
The Boy with the Lightning Feet
The Boy With the Magic Numbers
The Smallest Girl Ever
The Strongest Girl in the World

Lucy Willow

Wings & Co

Operation Bunny
Three Pickled Herrings
The Vanishing of Billy Buckle

For older readers

The Double Shadow
I, Coriander
The Red Necklace
The Silver Blade
Tinder

OLIVER TWIST

Charles Dickens

EDITORIAL DIRECTOR Justin Kestler
MANAGING EDITOR Ben Florman

SERIES EDITORS Boomie Aglietti, Justin Kestler
PRODUCTION Christian Lorentzen

WRITERS Valerie Jaffee, Selena Ward
EDITORS Benjamin Morgan, Dennis Quinio

This edition published by Spark Publishing

Spark Publishing
A Division of SparkNotes LLC
120 Fifth Avenue, 8th Floor
New York, NY 10011

02 03 04 05 SN 9 8 7 6 5 4 3 2 1

Please send all comments and questions or report errors to feedback@sparknotes.com.

Library of Congress information available upon request

Printed and bound in the United States

RRD-C

ISBN 1-58663-443-7

INTRODUCTION: STOPPING TO BUY SPARKNOTES ON A SNOWY EVENING

Whose words these are you *think* you know.
Your paper's due tomorrow, though;
We're glad to see you stopping here
To get some help before you go.

Lost your course? You'll find it here.
Face tests and essays without fear.
Between the words, good grades at stake:
Get great results throughout the year.

Once school bells caused your heart to quake
As teachers circled each mistake.
Use SparkNotes and no longer weep,
Ace every single test you take.

Yes, books are lovely, dark, and deep,
But only what you grasp you keep,
With hours to go before you sleep,
With hours to go before you sleep.

Contents

CONTEXT

C HARLES DICKENS WAS BORN on February 7, 1812, in Portsea, England. His parents were middle-class, but they suffered financially as a result of living beyond their means. When Dickens was twelve years old, his family's dire straits forced him to quit school and work in a blacking factory, a place where shoe polish is made. Within weeks, his father was put in debtor's prison, where Dickens's mother and siblings eventually joined him. At this point, Dickens lived on his own and continued to work at the factory for several months. The horrific conditions in the factory haunted him for the rest of his life, as did the experience of temporary orphanhood. Apparently, Dickens never forgot the day when a more senior boy in the warehouse took it upon himself to instruct Dickens in how to do his work more efficiently. For Dickens, that instruction may have represented the first step toward his full integration into the misery and tedium of working-class life. The more senior boy's name was Bob Fagin. Dickens's residual resentment of him reached a fevered pitch in the characterization of the villain Fagin in *Oliver Twist*.

After inheriting some money, Dickens's father got out of prison and Charles returned to school. As a young adult, he worked as a law clerk and later as a journalist. His experience as a journalist kept him in close contact with the darker social conditions of the Industrial Revolution, and he grew disillusioned with the attempts of lawmakers to alleviate those conditions. A collection of semi-fictional sketches entitled *Sketches by Boz* earned him recognition as a writer. Dickens became famous and began to make money from his writing when he published his first novel, *The Pickwick Papers,* which was serialized in 1836 and published in book form the following year.

In 1837, the first installment of *Oliver Twist* appeared in the magazine *Bentley's Miscellany,* which Dickens was then editing. It was accompanied by illustrations by George Cruikshank, which still accompany many editions of the novel today. Even at this early date, some critics accused Dickens of writing too quickly and too prolifically, since he was paid by the word for his serialized novels. Yet the passion behind *Oliver Twist,* animated in part by Dickens's own childhood experiences and in part by his outrage at the living conditions of the poor that he had witnessed as a journalist, touched his contemporary readers. Greatly successful, the novel was a thinly veiled protest against the Poor Law of 1834, which dictated that all public charity must be channeled through workhouses.

In 1836, Dickens married Catherine Hogarth, but after twenty years of marriage and ten children, he fell in love with Ellen Ternan, an actress many years his junior. Soon after, Dickens and his wife separated, ending a long series of marital difficulties. Dickens remained a prolific writer to the end of his life, and his novels—among them *Great Expectations, A Tale of Two Cities, A Christmas Carol, David Copperfield,* and *Bleak House*—continued to earn critical and popular acclaim. He died of a stroke in 1870, at the age of 58, leaving *The Mystery of Edwin Drood* unfinished.

THE POOR LAWS: *OLIVER TWIST*'S SOCIAL COMMENTARY

Oliver Twist opens with a bitter invective directed at the nineteenth-century English Poor Laws. These laws were a distorted manifestation of the Victorian middle class's emphasis on the virtues of hard work. England in the 1830s was rapidly undergoing a transformation from an agricultural, rural economy to an urban, industrial nation. The growing middle class had achieved an economic influence equal to, if not greater than, that of the British aristocracy.

In the 1830s, the middle class clamored for a share of political power with the landed gentry, bringing about a restructuring of the voting system. Parliament passed the Reform Act, which granted the right to vote to previously disenfranchised middle-class citizens. The middle class was eager to gain social legitimacy. This desire gave rise to the Evangelical religious movement and inspired sweeping economic and political change.

In the extremely stratified English class structure, the highest social class belonged to the "gentleman," an aristocrat who did not have to work for his living. The middle class was stigmatized for having to work, and so, to alleviate the stigma attached to middle-class wealth, the middle class promoted work as a moral virtue. But the resulting moral value attached to work, along with the middle class's insecurity about its own social legitimacy, led English society to subject the poor to hatred and cruelty. Many members of the middle class were anxious to be differentiated from the lower classes, and one way to do so was to stigmatize the lower classes as lazy good-for-nothings. The middle class's value system transformed earned

wealth into a sign of moral virtue. Victorian society interpreted economic success as a sign that God favored the honest, moral virtue of the successful individual's efforts, and, thus, interpreted the condition of poverty as a sign of the weakness of the poor individual.

The sentiment behind the Poor Law of 1834 reflected these beliefs. The law allowed the poor to receive public assistance only if they lived and worked in established workhouses. Beggars risked imprisonment. Debtors were sent to prison, often with their entire families, which virtually ensured that they could not repay their debts. Workhouses were deliberately made to be as miserable as possible in order to deter the poor from relying on public assistance. The philosophy was that the miserable conditions would prevent able-bodied paupers from being lazy and idle bums.

In the eyes of middle-class English society, those who could not support themselves were considered immoral and evil. Therefore, such individuals should enjoy no comforts or luxuries in their reliance on public assistance. In order to create the misery needed to deter immoral idleness, families were split apart upon entering the workhouse. Husbands were permitted no contact with their wives, lest they breed more paupers. Mothers were separated from children, lest they impart their immoral ways to their children. Brothers were separated from their sisters because the middle-class patrons of workhouses feared the lower class's "natural" inclination toward incest. In short, the state undertook to become the surrogate parents of workhouse children, whether or not they were orphans. Meals served to workhouse residents were deliberately inadequate, so as to encourage the residents to find work and support themselves.

Because of the great stigma attached to workhouse relief, many poor people chose to die in the streets rather than seek public aid. The workhouse was supposed to demonstrate the virtue of gainful employment to the poor. In order to receive public assistance, they had to pay in suffering and misery. Victorian values stressed the moral virtue of suffering and privation, and the workhouse residents were made to experience these virtues many times over.

Rather than improving what the middle class saw as the questionable morals of the able-bodied poor, the Poor Laws punished the most defenseless and helpless members of the lower class. The old, the sick, and the very young suffered more than the able-bodied benefited from these laws. Dickens meant to demonstrate this incongruity through the figure of Oliver Twist, an orphan born and raised in a workhouse for the first ten years of his life. His story demonstrates the hypocrisy of the petty middle-class bureaucrats, who treat a small child cruelly while voicing their belief in the Christian virtue of giving charity to the less fortunate.

Dickens was a lifelong champion of the poor. He himself suffered the harsh abuse visited upon the poor by the English legal system. In England in the 1830s, the poor truly had no voice, political or economic. In *Oliver Twist*, Dickens presents the everyday existence of the lowest members of English society. He goes far beyond the experiences of the workhouse, extending his depiction of poverty to London's squalid streets, dark alehouses, and thieves' dens. He gives voice to those who had no voice, establishing a link between politics and literature with his social commentary.

PLOT OVERVIEW

OLIVER TWIST IS BORN in a workhouse in 1830s England. His mother, whose name no one knows, is found on the street and dies just after Oliver's birth. Oliver spends the first nine years of his life in a badly run home for young orphans and then is transferred to a workhouse for adults. After the other boys bully Oliver into asking for more gruel at the end of a meal, Mr. Bumble, the parish beadle, offers five pounds to anyone who will take the boy away from the workhouse. Oliver narrowly escapes being apprenticed to a brutish chimney sweep and is eventually apprenticed to a local undertaker, Mr. Sowerberry. When the undertaker's other apprentice, Noah Claypole, makes disparaging comments about Oliver's mother, Oliver attacks him and incurs the Sowerberrys' wrath. Desperate, Oliver runs away at dawn and travels toward London.

Outside London, Oliver, starved and exhausted, meets Jack Dawkins, a boy his own age. Jack offers him shelter in the London house of his benefactor, Fagin. It turns out that Fagin is a career criminal who trains orphan boys to pick pockets for him. After a few days of training, Oliver is sent on a pickpocketing mission with two other boys. When he sees them swipe a handkerchief from an elderly gentleman, Oliver is horrified and runs off. He is caught but narrowly escapes being convicted of the theft. Mr. Brownlow, the man whose handkerchief was stolen, takes the feverish Oliver to his home and nurses him back to health. Mr. Brownlow is struck by Oliver's resemblance to a portrait of a young woman that hangs in his house. Oliver thrives in Mr. Brownlow's home, but two young adults in Fagin's gang, Bill Sikes and his lover Nancy, capture Oliver and return him to Fagin.

Fagin sends Oliver to assist Sikes in a burglary. Oliver is shot by a servant of the house and, after Sikes escapes, is taken in by the women who live there, Mrs. Maylie and her beautiful adopted niece Rose. They grow fond of Oliver, and he spends an idyllic summer with them in the countryside. But Fagin and a mysterious man named Monks are set on recapturing Oliver. Meanwhile, it is revealed that Oliver's mother left behind a gold locket when she died. Monks obtains and destroys that locket. When the Maylies come to London, Nancy meets secretly with Rose and informs her

5

of Fagin's designs, but a member of Fagin's gang overhears the conversation. When word of Nancy's disclosure reaches Sikes, he brutally murders Nancy and flees London. Pursued by his guilty conscience and an angry mob, he inadvertently hangs himself while trying to escape.

Mr. Brownlow, with whom the Maylies have reunited Oliver, confronts Monks and wrings the truth about Oliver's parentage from him. It is revealed that Monks is Oliver's half brother. Their father, Mr. Leeford, was unhappily married to a wealthy woman and had an affair with Oliver's mother, Agnes Fleming. Monks has been pursuing Oliver all along in the hopes of ensuring that his half-brother is deprived of his share of the family inheritance. Mr. Brownlow forces Monks to sign over Oliver's share to Oliver. Moreover, it is discovered that Rose is Agnes's younger sister, hence Oliver's aunt. Fagin is hung for his crimes. Finally, Mr. Brownlow adopts Oliver, and they and the Maylies retire to a blissful existence in the countryside.

CHARACTER LIST

Oliver Twist The novel's protagonist. Oliver is an orphan born in a workhouse, and Dickens uses his situation to criticize public policy toward the poor in 1830s England. Oliver is between nine and twelve years old when the main action of the novel occurs. Though treated with cruelty and surrounded by coarseness for most of his life, he is a pious, innocent child, and his charms draw the attention of several wealthy benefactors. His true identity is the central mystery of the novel.

Fagin   A conniving career criminal. Fagin takes in homeless children and trains them to pick pockets for him. He is also a buyer of other people's stolen goods. He rarely commits crimes himself, preferring to employ others to commit them—and often suffer legal retribution—in his place. Dickens's portrait of Fagin displays the influence of anti-Semitic stereotypes.

Nancy   A young prostitute and one of Fagin's former child pickpockets. Nancy is also Bill Sikes's lover. Her love for Sikes and her sense of moral decency come into conflict when Sikes abuses Oliver. Despite her criminal lifestyle, she is among the noblest characters in the novel. In effect, she gives her life for Oliver when Sikes murders her for revealing Monks's plots.

Rose Maylie Agnes Fleming's sister, raised by Mrs. Maylie after the death of Rose's father. A beautiful, compassionate, and forgiving young woman, Rose is the novel's model of female virtue. She establishes a loving relationship with Oliver even before it is revealed that the two are related.

Mr. Brownlow A well-off, erudite gentleman who serves as Oliver's first benefactor. Mr. Brownlow owns a portrait of Agnes Fleming and was engaged to Mr. Leeford's sister when she died. Throughout the novel, he behaves with compassion and common sense and emerges as a natural leader.

Monks A sickly, vicious young man, prone to violent fits and teeming with inexplicable hatred. With Fagin, he schemes to give Oliver a bad reputation.

Bill Sikes A brutal professional burglar brought up in Fagin's gang. Sikes and Nancy are lovers, and he treats both her and his dog Bull's-eye with an odd combination of cruelty and grudging familiarity. His murder of Nancy is the most heinous of the many crimes that occur in the novel.

Mr. Bumble The pompous, self-important beadle—a minor church official—for the workhouse where Oliver is born. Though Mr. Bumble preaches Christian morality, he behaves without compassion toward the paupers under his care. Dickens mercilessly satirizes his self-righteousness, greed, hypocrisy, and folly, of which his name is an obvious symbol.

Agnes Fleming Oliver's mother. After falling in love with and becoming pregnant by Mr. Leeford, she chooses to die anonymously in a workhouse rather than stain her family's reputation. A retired naval officer's daughter, she was a beautiful, loving woman. Oliver's face closely resembles hers.

Mr. Leeford Oliver and Monks's father, who dies long before the events of the novel. He was an intelligent, high-minded man whose family forced him into an unhappy marriage with a wealthy woman. He eventually separated from his wife and had an illicit love affair with Agnes Fleming. He intended to flee the country with Agnes but died before he could do so.

Mr. Losberne Mrs. Maylie's family physician. A hot-tempered but good-hearted old bachelor, Mr. Losberne is fiercely loyal to the Maylies and, eventually, to Oliver.

Mrs. Maylie A kind, wealthy older woman, the mother of Harry Maylie and adoptive "aunt" of Rose.

Harry Maylie Mrs. Maylie's son. Harry is a dashing young man with grand political ambitions and career prospects, which he eventually gives up to marry Rose.

The Artful Dodger The cleverest of Fagin's pickpockets. The Dodger's real name is Jack Dawkins. Though no older than Oliver, the Dodger talks and dresses like a grown man. He introduces Oliver to Fagin.

Charley Bates One of Fagin's pickpockets. Charley is ready to laugh at anything.

Old Sally An elderly pauper who serves as the nurse at Oliver's birth. Old Sally steals Agnes's gold locket, the only clue to Oliver's identity.

Mrs. Corney The matron of the workhouse where Oliver is born. Mrs. Corney is hypocritical, callous, and materialistic. After she marries Mr. Bumble, she hounds him mercilessly.

Noah Claypole A charity boy and Mr. Sowerberry's apprentice. Noah is an overgrown, cowardly bully who mistreats Oliver and eventually joins Fagin's gang.

Charlotte The Sowerberrys' maid. Charlotte becomes romantically involved with Noah Claypole and follows him about slavishly.

Toby Crackit One of Fagin and Sikes's associates, crass and not too bright. Toby participates in the attempted burglary of Mrs. Maylie's home.

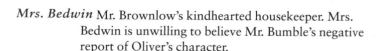

Mrs. Bedwin Mr. Brownlow's kindhearted housekeeper. Mrs. Bedwin is unwilling to believe Mr. Bumble's negative report of Oliver's character.

Bull's-eye Bill Sikes's dog. As vicious as his master, Bull's-eye functions as Sikes's alter ego.

Monks's mother An heiress who lived a decadent life and alienated her husband, Mr. Leeford. Monks's mother destroyed Mr. Leeford's will, which left part of his property to Oliver. Much of Monks's nastiness is presumably inherited from her.

Mr. Sowerberry The undertaker to whom Oliver is apprenticed. Though Mr. Sowerberry makes a grotesque living arranging cut-rate burials for paupers, he is a decent man who is kind to Oliver.

Mrs. Sowerberry Sowerberry's wife. Mrs. Sowerberry is a mean, judgmental woman who henpecks her husband.

Mr. Grimwig Brownlow's pessimistic, curmudgeonly friend. Mr. Grimwig is essentially good-hearted, and his pessimism is mostly just a provocative character quirk.

Mr. Giles Mrs. Maylie's loyal, though somewhat pompous, butler.

Mr. Brittles A sort of handyman for Mrs. Maylie's estate. It is implied that Mr. Brittles is slightly mentally handicapped.

Mrs. Mann The superintendent of the juvenile workhouse where Oliver is raised. Mrs. Mann physically abuses and half-starves the children in her care.

Mr. Gamfield A brutal chimney sweep. Oliver almost becomes Mr. Gamfield's apprentice.

Bet One of Fagin's former child pickpockets, now a prostitute.

Mr. Fang   The harsh, irrational, power-hungry magistrate who presides over Oliver's trial for pickpocketing.

Barney   One of Fagin's criminal associates. Like Fagin, Barney is Jewish.

Duff and Blathers Two bumbling police officers who investigate the attempted burglary of Mrs. Maylie's home.

Tom Chitling A rather dim member of Fagin's gang. Tom has served time in jail for doing Fagin's bidding.

ANALYSIS OF MAJOR CHARACTERS

OLIVER TWIST

As the child hero of a melodramatic novel of social protest, Oliver Twist is meant to appeal more to our sentiments than to our literary sensibilities. On many levels, Oliver is not a believable character, because although he is raised in corrupt surroundings, his purity and virtue are absolute. Throughout the novel, Dickens uses Oliver's character to challenge the Victorian idea that paupers and criminals are already evil at birth, arguing instead that a corrupt environment is the source of vice. At the same time, Oliver's incorruptibility undermines some of Dickens's assertions. Oliver is shocked and horrified when he sees the Artful Dodger and Charley Bates pick a stranger's pocket and again when he is forced to participate in a burglary. Oliver's moral scruples about the sanctity of property seem inborn in him, just as Dickens's opponents thought that corruption is inborn in poor people. Furthermore, other pauper children use rough Cockney slang, but Oliver, oddly enough, speaks in proper King's English. His grammatical fastidiousness is also inexplicable, as Oliver presumably is not well-educated. Even when he is abused and manipulated, Oliver does not become angry or indignant. When Sikes and Crackit force him to assist in a robbery, Oliver merely begs to be allowed to "run away and die in the fields." Oliver does not present a complex picture of a person torn between good and evil—instead, he is goodness incarnate.

Even if we might feel that Dickens's social criticism would have been more effective if he had focused on a more complex poor character, like the Artful Dodger or Nancy, the audience for whom Dickens was writing might not have been receptive to such a portrayal. Dickens's Victorian middle-class readers were likely to hold opinions on the poor that were only a little less extreme than those expressed by Mr. Bumble, the beadle who treats paupers with great cruelty. In fact, *Oliver Twist* was criticized for portraying thieves and prostitutes at all. Given the strict morals of Dickens's audience, it may have seemed necessary for him to make Oliver a saintlike figure. Because Oliver appealed to Victorian readers' sentiments, his story may have stood a better chance of effectively challenging their prejudices.

NANCY

A major concern of *Oliver Twist* is the question of whether a bad environment can irrevocably poison someone's character and soul. As the novel progresses, the character who best illustrates the contradictory issues brought up by that question is Nancy. As a child of the streets, Nancy has been a thief and drinks to excess. The narrator's reference to her "free and agreeable . . . manners" indicates that she is a prostitute. She is immersed in the vices condemned by her society, but she also commits perhaps the most noble act in the novel when she sacrifices her own life in order to protect Oliver. Nancy's moral complexity is unique among the major characters in *Oliver Twist*. The novel is full of characters who are all good and can barely comprehend evil, such as Oliver, Rose, and Brownlow; and characters who are all evil and can barely comprehend good, such as Fagin, Sikes, and Monks. Only Nancy comprehends and is capable of both good and evil. Her ultimate choice to do good at a great personal cost is a strong argument in favor of the incorruptibility of basic goodness, no matter how many environmental obstacles it may face.

Nancy's love for Sikes exemplifies the moral ambiguity of her character. As she herself points out to Rose, devotion to a man can be "a comfort and a pride" under the right circumstances. But for Nancy, such devotion is "a new means of violence and suffering"—indeed, her relationship with Sikes leads her to criminal acts for his sake and eventually to her own demise. The same behavior, in different circumstances, can have very different consequences and moral significance. In much of *Oliver Twist,* morality and nobility are black-and-white issues, but Nancy's character suggests that the boundary between virtue and vice is not always clearly drawn.

FAGIN

Although Dickens denied that anti-Semitism had influenced his portrait of Fagin, the Jewish thief's characterization does seem to owe much to ethnic stereotypes. He is ugly, simpering, miserly, and avaricious. Constant references to him as "the Jew" seem to indicate that his negative traits are intimately connected to his ethnic identity. However, Fagin is more than a statement of ethnic prejudice. He is a richly drawn, resonant embodiment of terrifying villainy. At times, he seems like a child's distorted vision of pure evil. Fagin is described as a "loathsome reptile" and as having "fangs such as should have been a dog's or rat's." Other characters occasionally refer to him as "the old one," a popular nickname for the devil. Twice, in Chapter 9 and again in Chapter 34, Oliver wakes up to find Fagin nearby. Oliver encounters him in the hazy zone between sleep and waking, at the precise time when dreams and nightmares are born from "the mere silent presence of some external object." Indeed, Fagin is meant to inspire nightmares in child and adult readers alike. Perhaps most frightening of all, though, is Chapter 52, in which we enter Fagin's head for his "last night alive." The gallows, and the fear they inspire in Fagin, are a specter even more horrifying to contemplate than Fagin himself.

CHARACTER ANALYSIS

Themes, Motifs & Symbols

Themes

Themes are the fundamental and often universal ideas explored in a literary work.

The Failure of Charity

Much of the first part of *Oliver Twist* challenges the organizations of charity run by the church and the government in Dickens's time. The system Dickens describes was put into place by the Poor Law of 1834, which stipulated that the poor could only receive government assistance if they moved into government workhouses. Residents of those workhouses were essentially inmates whose rights were severely curtailed by a host of onerous regulations. Labor was required, families were almost always separated, and rations of food and clothing were meager. The workhouses operated on the principle that poverty was the consequence of laziness and that the dreadful conditions in the workhouse would inspire the poor to better their own circumstances. Yet the economic dislocation of the Industrial Revolution made it impossible for many to do so, and the workhouses did not provide any means for social or economic betterment. Furthermore, as Dickens points out, the officials who ran the workhouses blatantly violated the values they preached to the poor. Dickens describes with great sarcasm the greed, laziness, and arrogance of charitable workers like Mr. Bumble and Mrs. Mann. In general, charitable institutions only reproduced the awful conditions in which the poor would live anyway. As Dickens puts it, the poor choose between "being starved by a gradual process in the house, or by a quick one out of it."

The Folly of Individualism

With the rise of capitalism during the Industrial Revolution, individualism was very much in vogue as a philosophy. Victorian capitalists believed that society would run most smoothly if individuals looked out for their own interests. Ironically, the clearest pronunciation of this philosophy comes not from a legitimate businessman but from Fagin, who operates in the illicit businesses of theft and prostitution. He tells Noah Claypole that "a regard for number one holds us all together, and must do so, unless we would all go to pieces in company." In other words, the group's interests are best maintained if every individual looks out for "number one," or himself. The folly of this philosophy is demonstrated at the end of the novel, when Nancy turns against Monks, Charley Bates turns against Sikes, and Monks turns against Mrs. Corney. Fagin's unstable family, held together only by the self-interest of its members, is juxtaposed to the little society formed by Oliver, Brownlow, Rose Maylie, and their many friends. This second group is bound together not by concerns of self-interest but by "strong affection and humanity of heart," the selfless devotion to each other that Dickens sees as the prerequisite for "perfect happiness."

Purity in a Corrupt City

Throughout the novel, Dickens confronts the question of whether the terrible environments he depicts have the power to "blacken [the soul] and change its hue for ever." By examining the fates of most of the characters, we can assume that his answer is that they do not. Certainly, characters like Sikes and Fagin seem to have sustained permanent damage to their moral sensibilities. Yet even Sikes has a conscience, which manifests itself in the apparition of Nancy's eyes that haunts him after he murders her. Charley Bates maintains enough of a sense of decency to try to capture Sikes. Of course, Oliver is above any corruption, though the novel removes him from unhealthy environments relatively early in his life. Most telling of all is Nancy, who, though she considers herself "lost almost beyond redemption," ends up making the ultimate sacrifice for a child she hardly knows. In contrast, Monks, perhaps the novel's most inhuman villain, was brought up amid wealth and comfort.

The Countryside Idealized

All the injustices and privations suffered by the poor in *Oliver Twist* occur in cities—either the great city of London or the provincial city where Oliver is born. When the Maylies take Oliver to the countryside, he discovers a "new existence." Dickens asserts that even people who have spent their entire lives in "close and noisy places" are likely, in the last moments of their lives, to find comfort in half-imagined memories "of sky, and hill and plain." Moreover, country scenes have the potential to "purify our thoughts" and erase some of the vices that develop in the city. Hence, in the country, "the poor people [are] so neat and clean," living a life that is free of the squalor that torments their urban counterparts. Oliver and his new family settle in a small village at the novel's end, as if a happy ending would not be possible in the city. Dickens's portrait of rural life in *Oliver Twist* is more approving yet far less realistic than his portrait of urban life. This fact does not contradict, but rather supports, the general estimation of Dickens as a great urban writer. It is precisely Dickens's distance from the countryside that allows him to idealize it.

MOTIFS

Motifs are recurring structures, contrasts, or literary devices that can help to develop and inform the text's major themes.

DISGUISED OR MISTAKEN IDENTITIES

The plot of *Oliver Twist* revolves around the various false identities that other characters impose upon Oliver, often for the sake of advancing their own interests. Mr. Bumble and the other workhouse officials insist on portraying Oliver as something he is not—an ungrateful, immoral pauper. Monks does his best to conceal Oliver's real identity so that Monks himself can claim Oliver's rightful inheritance. Characters also disguise their own identities when it serves them well to do so. Nancy pretends to be Oliver's middle-class sister in order to get him back to Fagin, while Monks changes his name and poses as a common criminal rather than the heir he really is. Scenes depicting the manipulation of clothing indicate how it plays an important part in the construction of various characters' identities. Nancy dons new clothing to pass as a middle-class girl, and Fagin strips Oliver of all his upper-class credibility when he takes from him the suit of clothes purchased by Brownlow. The novel's resolution revolves around the revelation of the real identities of Oliver, Rose, and Monks. Only when every character's identity is known with certainty does the story achieve real closure.

HIDDEN FAMILY RELATIONSHIPS

The revelation of Oliver's familial ties is among the novel's most unlikely plot turns: Oliver is related to Brownlow, who was married to his father's sister; to Rose, who is his aunt; and to Monks, who is his half-brother. The coincidences involved in these facts are quite unbelievable and represent the novel's rejection of realism in favor of fantasy. Oliver is at first believed to be an orphan without parents or relatives, a position that would, in that time and place, almost certainly seal his doom. Yet, by the end of the novel, it is revealed that he has more relatives than just about anyone else in the novel. This reversal of his fortunes strongly resembles the fulfillment of a naïve child's wish. It also suggests the mystical binding power of family relationships. Brownlow and Rose take to Oliver immediately, even though he is implicated in an attempted robbery of Rose's house, while Monks recognizes Oliver the instant he sees him on the street. The influence of blood ties, it seems, can be felt even before anyone knows those ties exist.

SURROGATE FAMILIES

Before Oliver finds his real family, a number of individuals serve him as substitue parents, mostly with very limited success. Mrs. Mann and Mr. Bumble are surrogate parents, albeit horribly negligent ones, for the vast numbers of orphans under their care. Mr. Sowerberry and his wife, while far from ideal, are much more serviceable parent figures to Oliver, and one can even imagine that Oliver might have grown up to be a productive citizen under their care. Interestingly, it is the mention of his real mother that leads to Oliver's voluntary abandonment of the Sowerberrys. The most provocative of the novel's mock family structures is the unit formed by Fagin and his young charges. Fagin provides for and trains his wards nearly as well as a father might, and he inspires enough loyalty in them that they stick around even after they are grown. But these quasi-familial relationships are built primarily around exploitation and not out of true concern or selfless interest. Oddly enough, the only satisfactory surrogate parents Oliver finds are Brownlow and Rose, both of whom turn out to be actual relatives.

OLIVER'S FACE

Oliver's face is singled out for special attention at multiple points in the novel. Mr. Sowerberry, Charley Bates, and Toby Crackit all comment on its particular appeal, and its resemblance to the portrait of Agnes Fleming provides the first clue to Oliver's identity. The power of Oliver's physiognomy, combined with the facts that Fagin is hideous and Rose is beautiful, suggests that in the world of the novel, external appearance usually gives a fair impression of a person's inner character.

SYMBOLS

Symbols are objects, characters, figures, or colors used to represent abstract ideas or concepts.

CHARACTERS' NAMES

The names of characters represent personal qualities. Oliver Twist himself is the most obvious example. The name "Twist," though given by accident, alludes to the outrageous reversals of fortune that he will experience. Rose Maylie's name echoes her association with flowers and springtime, youth and beauty. Toby Crackit's name is a lighthearted reference to his chosen profession of breaking into houses. Mr. Bumble's name connotes his bumbling arrogance; Mrs. Mann's, her lack of maternal instinct; and Mr. Grimwig's, his superficial grimness that can be removed as easily as a wig.

BULL'S-EYE

Bill Sikes's dog, Bull's-eye, has "faults of temper in common with his owner" and is a symbolic emblem of his owner's character. The dog's viciousness reflects and represents Sikes's own animal-like brutality. After Sikes murders Nancy, Bull's-eye comes to represent Sikes's guilt. The dog leaves bloody footprints on the floor of the room where the murder is committed. Not long after, Sikes becomes desperate to get rid of the dog, convinced that the dog's presence will give him away. Yet, just as Sikes cannot shake off his guilt, he cannot shake off Bull's-eye, who arrives at the house of Sikes's demise before Sikes himself does. Bull's-eye's name also conjures up the image of Nancy's eyes, which haunts Sikes until the bitter end and eventually causes him to hang himself accidentally.

LONDON BRIDGE

Nancy's decision to meet Brownlow and Rose on London Bridge reveals the symbolic aspect of this bridge in *Oliver Twist*. Bridges exist to link two places that would otherwise be separated by an uncrossable chasm. The meeting on London Bridge represents the collision of two worlds unlikely ever to come into contact—the idyllic world of Brownlow and Rose, and the atmosphere of degradation in which Nancy lives. On the bridge, Nancy is given the chance to cross over to the better way of life that the others represent, but she rejects that opportunity, and by the time the three have all left the bridge, that possibility has vanished forever.

Summary & Analysis

Chapters 1–4

Summary: Chapter 1

Oliver Twist is born a sickly infant in a workhouse. The parish surgeon and a drunken nurse attend his birth. His mother kisses his forehead and dies, and the nurse announces that Oliver's mother was found lying in the streets the night before. The surgeon notices that she is not wearing a wedding ring.

Summary: Chapter 2

> *So they established the rule that all poor people*
> *should have the alternative . . . of being starved by a*
> *gradual process in the house, or by a quick one out*
> *of it.*   (See QUOTATIONS, p. 61)

Authorities at the workhouse send Oliver to a branch-workhouse for "juvenile offenders against the poor-laws." The overseer, Mrs. Mann, receives an adequate sum for each child's upkeep, but she keeps most of the money and lets the children go hungry, sometimes even letting them die.

On Oliver's ninth birthday, Mr. Bumble, a minor church official known as the parish beadle, informs Mrs. Mann that Oliver is too old to stay at her establishment. Since no one has been able to discover his mother's or father's identity, he must return to the workhouse. Mrs. Mann asks how the boy came to have any name at all. Mr. Bumble tells her that he keeps a list of names in alphabetical order, naming the orphans from the list as they are born.

Mrs. Mann fetches Oliver. When Mr. Bumble is not looking, she glowers and shakes her fist at the boy, so he stays silent about the miserable conditions at her establishment. Before Oliver departs, Mrs. Mann gives him some bread and butter so that he will not seem too hungry at the workhouse.

The workhouse offers the poor the opportunity to starve slowly as opposed to quick starvation on the streets. For the workhouse, the undertaker's bill is a major budget item due to the large number of deaths. Oliver and his young companions suffer the "tortures of slow starvation." One night at dinner, one child tells the others that if he does not have another bowl of gruel he might eat one of them. Terrified, the children at the workhouse cast lots, determining that whoever loses shall be required to ask for more food for the boy. Oliver loses, and after dinner, the other children insist that Oliver ask for more food at supper. His request so shocks the authorities that they offer five pounds as a reward to anyone who will take Oliver off of their hands.

SUMMARY: CHAPTER 3

In the parish, Oliver has been flogged and then locked in a dark room as a public example. Mr. Gamfield, a brutish chimney sweep, offers to take Oliver on as an apprentice. Because several boys have died under his supervision, the board considers five pounds too large a reward, and they settle on just over three pounds. Mr. Bumble, Mr. Gamfield, and Oliver appear before a magistrate to seal the bargain. At the last minute, the magistrate notices Oliver's pale, alarmed face. He asks the boy why he looks so terrified. Oliver falls on his knees and begs that he be locked in a room, beaten, killed, or any other punishment besides being apprenticed to Mr. Gamfield. The magistrate refuses to approve the apprenticeship, and the workhouse authorities again advertise Oliver's availability.

SUMMARY: CHAPTER 4

The workhouse board considers sending Oliver out to sea as a cabin boy, expecting that he would die quickly in such miserable conditions. However, Mr. Sowerberry, the parish undertaker, takes Oliver on as his apprentice. Mr. Bumble informs Oliver that he will suffer dire consequences if he ever complains about his situation. Mrs. Sowerberry remarks that Oliver is rather small. Mr. Bumble assures her that he will grow, but she grumbles that he will only grow by eating their food. Mrs. Sowerberry serves Oliver the leftovers that the dog has declined to eat. Oliver devours the food as though it were a great feast. After he finishes, Mrs. Sowerberry leads him to his bed, worrying that his appetite seems so large.

ANALYSIS: CHAPTERS 1–4

Oliver Twist is an extreme criticism of Victorian society's treatment of the poor. The workhouses that figure prominently in the first few chapters of the novel were institutions that the Victorian middle class established to raise poor children. Since it was believed that certain vices were inherent to the poor and that poor families fostered rather than discouraged such vices, poor husbands and wives were separated in order to prevent them from having children and expanding the lower class. Poor children were taken away from their parents in order to allow the state and the church to raise them in the manner they believed most appropriate.

In the narrative, the workhouse functions as a sign of the moral hypocrisy of the working class. Mrs. Mann steals from the children in her care, feeding and clothing them inadequately. The Victorian middle class saw cleanliness as a moral virtue, and the workhouse was supposed to rescue the poor from the immoral condition of filth. However, the workhouse in Dickens's novel is a filthy place—Mrs. Mann never ensures that the children practice good hygiene except during an inspection. Workhouses were established to save the poor from starvation, disease, and filth, but in fact they end up visiting precisely those hardships on the poor. Furthermore, Mr. Bumble's actions underscore middle-class hypocrisy, especially when he criticizes Oliver for not gratefully accepting his dire conditions. Bumble himself, however, is fat and well-dressed, and the entire workhouse board is full of fat gentlemen who preach the value of a meager diet for workhouse residents.

The assumption on the part of the middle-class characters that the lower classes are naturally base, criminal, and filthy serves to support their vision of themselves as a clean and morally upright social group. The gentlemen on the workhouse board call Oliver a "savage" who is destined for the gallows. After Oliver's outrageous request for more food, the board schemes to apprentice him to a brutal master, hoping that he will soon die. Even when the upper classes claim to be alleviating the lower-class predicament, they only end up aggravating it. In order to save Oliver from what they believe to be his certain fate as a criminal, the board essentially ensures his early death by apprenticing him to a brutal employer.

The workhouse reproduces the vices it is supposed to erase. One workhouse boy, with a "wild, hungry" look, threatens in jest to eat another boy. The suggestion is that workhouses force their residents to become cannibals. The workhouse also mimics the institution of slavery: the residents are fed and clothed as little as possible and required to work at tasks assigned by the board, and they are required to put on a face of cheery, grateful acceptance of the miserable conditions that have been forced on them. When Oliver does not, he is sold rather than sent away freely.

Dickens achieves his biting criticism of social conditions through deep satire and hyperbolic statements. Throughout the novel, absurd characters and situations are presented as normal, and Dickens often says the opposite of what he really means. For example, in describing the men of the parish board, Dickens writes that "they were very sage, deep, philosophical men" who discover about the workhouse that "the poor people liked it! It was a regular place of public entertainment for the poorer classes; a tavern where there was nothing to pay. . . ." Of course, we know that Oliver's experience with the workhouse is anything but entertaining and that the men of the parish board are anything but "sage, deep," or "philosophical." But by making statements such as these, Dickens highlights the comical extent to which the upper classes are willfully ignorant of the plight of the lower classes. Since paupers like Oliver stand no chance of defeating their tormentors, Dickens takes it upon himself to defeat them with sly humor that reveals their faults more sharply than a serious tone might have. Though Oliver himself will never have much of a sense of humor, we will eventually meet other boys in his situation who will join Dickens in using humor as a weapon in their woefully unequal struggle with the society that oppresses them.

CHAPTERS 5–8

SUMMARY: CHAPTER 5

In the morning, Noah Claypole, Mr. Sowerberry's apprentice, wakes Oliver. Noah and Charlotte, the maid, taunt Oliver during breakfast. Oliver accompanies Sowerberry to prepare for a pauper's burial. The husband of the deceased delivers a tearful tirade against his wife's death. She has starved to death, and although he once tried to beg for her, the authorities sent him to prison for the offense. The dead woman's mother begs for some bread and a cloak to wear for the funeral.

At the graveyard before the funeral, some ragged boys jump back and forth over the coffin to amuse themselves. Mr. Bumble beats a few of the boys. The clergyman performs the service in four minutes. Mr. Bumble quickly ushers the grieving family out of the cemetery, and Mr. Sowerberry takes the cloak away from the dead woman's mother. Oliver decides that he is not at all fond of the undertaking business.

Summary: Chapter 6

A measles epidemic arrives, and Oliver gains extensive experience in undertaking. His master dresses him well so that he can march in the processions. Oliver notes that the relatives of deceased, wealthy, elderly people quickly overcome their grief after the funeral.

Noah becomes increasingly jealous of Oliver's speedy advancement. One day, he insults Oliver's dead mother. Oliver attacks him in a fit of rage. Charlotte and Mrs. Sowerberry rush to Noah's aid, and the three of them beat Oliver and lock him in the cellar.

Summary: Chapter 7

Noah rushes to fetch Mr. Bumble, sobbing so that his injuries from his confrontation with Oliver appear much worse than they are. Mr. Bumble informs Mrs. Sowerberry that feeding meat to Oliver gives him more spirit than is appropriate to his station in life. Still enraged, Oliver kicks at the cellar door. Sowerberry returns home, beats Oliver, and locks him up again. Oliver's rage dissolves into tears. Early the next morning, Oliver runs away. On his way out of town, he passes the workhouse where he used to live and sees an old friend, Dick, in the yard. Dick vows not to tell anyone about Oliver's flight and bids him a warm farewell.

Summary: Chapter 8

Oliver decides to walk the seventy miles to London. Hunger, cold, and fatigue weaken him over the next seven days. In one village, signs warn that beggars will be thrown in jail. Finally, Oliver limps into a small town just outside London and collapses in a doorway. He is approached by a boy about his own age named Jack Dawkins, who dresses and acts like a grown man. Jack purchases a large lunch for Oliver and informs him that he knows a "genelman" in London who will let Oliver stay in his home for free. Oliver learns that Jack's nickname is "the Artful Dodger." He guesses from the Dodger's appearance that his way of life is immoral. He plans to ingratiate himself with the gentleman in London and then end all association with Jack.

That night, the Dodger takes Oliver to a squalid London neighborhood. At a dilapidated house, the Dodger calls out a password, and a man allows them to enter. The Dodger conducts Oliver into a filthy, black back room where an "old shrivelled Jew" named Fagin and some boys are having supper. Silk handkerchiefs hang everywhere. The boys smoke pipes and drink liquor although none appear older than the Dodger. Oliver takes a share of the dinner and sinks into a deep sleep.

ANALYSIS: CHAPTERS 5–8

Noah Claypole's relationship with Oliver illustrates Victorian England's obsession with class distinctions. The son of destitute parents, Noah is accustomed to the disdain of those who are better off than he. Thus, he is relieved to have Oliver nearby, since, as an orphan, Oliver is even worse off than he is. Dickens characterizes Noah's cowardice and bullying as "the same amiable qualities" that are "developed in the finest lord." Dickens shows that class snobbery is a universal quality, characteristic of the lowest as well as the highest strata of society. Moreover, snobbish behavior seems a component of class insecurity. The poor mercilessly taunt those who are poorer than they, out of anxious desire to distinguish themselves from those who are even worse off in life.

In protesting the parish's treatment of Oliver, Dickens criticizes the Victorian characterization of the poor as naturally immoral, criminal, and filthy. His principal character, Oliver, after all, is virtuous, good, and innocent. Although we might expect a criticism of the popular conception of the lower classes to describe many lower-class characters who are essentially good, honest, and hardworking, Dickens does not paint such a simplistic picture. The character of Noah, for example, exhibits the same stereotypes that Dickens satirizes in the first several chapters. Noah, the son of a drunkard, seems to have inherited all of the unpleasant traits that his father presumably has. Big, greedy, cowardly, ugly, and dirty, Noah is the quintessential Victorian stereotype of the good-for-nothing poor man.

Part of Dickens's motivation for writing *Oliver Twist* was to expose the horrid conditions in which the lower classes were expected to live, and, as a result, much of the narrative focuses on the sensationally disgusting settings in which the poor live their lives. At one point, Oliver and Sowerberry travel to a squalid section of town to retrieve a dead pauper's body. The neighborhood is full of shop fronts that are "fast closed and mouldering away." The people of this neighborhood have apparently been left behind by the economic expansion of the Industrial Revolution, which was in full force at the time of *Oliver Twist*'s publication. The bereaved husband's wife does not starve to death as a result of her "natural" laziness—she starves to death because of the economic realities of the society in which she lives.

Oliver's attack on Noah is an important moment in the development of his character. Most of the time, he is portrayed as sweet, docile, innocent, and naïve—sometimes to the point of seeming somewhat dim. Indeed, it might seem that Dickens, in his fervent desire to exact his Victorian audience's sympathy for the poor orphan, exaggerates by making Oliver angelic. Oliver's fit of rage, however, makes him seem more passionate and human, like an ordinary child. Oliver, raised in the workhouse, has never seen a functioning family except for the Sowerberrys, who are childless. His sense of familial love and duty is strong enough to compel him to violently come to his mother's defense. Dickens implies that loyalty to kin, and the desire for the love of a family, is an impulse with which children are born, not one that needs to be learned and nurtured.

Oliver's trip to London parallels the migration of the poor to the urban centers of England during the Industrial Revolution. His hungry, exhausted condition is a result of the laws forbidding begging, and it leaves him vulnerable enough to accept the questionable charity of a band of thieves. Dickens clearly blames the crimes committed by the poor on the people who passed the draconian Poor Laws. Thus, in order to survive, Oliver must accept the aid of Fagin's band. Oliver's stay with Fagin's band represents the first truly domestic experience in his life. Although Fagin's house is filthy and derelict, it contains a relatively idyllic dinner scene, with plenty of food laid out in pewter dishes and no one to begrudge Oliver his full share of the food.

CHAPTERS 9–12

SUMMARY: CHAPTER 9

The next morning, Fagin takes out a box full of jewelry and watches. He notices Oliver observing him. Fagin grabs a bread knife and asks Oliver if he was awake an hour before. Oliver says he was not, and Fagin regains his kindly demeanor.

The Artful Dodger returns with another boy, named Charley Bates. Fagin asks if they worked hard that morning. The Dodger produces two pocketbooks, and Charley pulls out four handkerchiefs. Fagin says that they will have to teach Oliver how to pick out the marks on the handkerchiefs with a needle. Oliver does not realize he has joined a band of pickpockets, so he believes their jokes about teaching him how to make handkerchiefs and pocketbooks.

Dodger and Charley practice picking Fagin's pockets. Two young women, Bet and Nancy, whom the narrator describes as "remarkably free and agreeable," drop in for drinks. Fagin gives all of them some money and sends them out. Fagin lets Oliver practice taking a handkerchief out of his pocket and gives him a shilling for a job well done.

Summary: Chapter 10

For days, Fagin keeps Oliver indoors practicing the art of picking pockets. Oliver notices that Fagin punishes the Dodger and Charley if they return home empty-handed. Finally, Fagin sends Oliver out with the Dodger and Charley to "work."

After some time, the Dodger notices a wealthy gentleman absorbed in reading at a bookstall. Oliver watches with horror as Charley and the Dodger sneak up behind the man and steal his handkerchief. He finally understands the nature of Fagin's work.

The gentleman turns and sees Oliver running away. Thinking that Oliver is the thief, he raises a cry. The Dodger and Charley see Oliver running past them, so they join in, crying, "Stop thief!" A large crowd joins the pursuit. A police officer arrives and grabs Oliver by the collar, ignoring the boy's protests of his innocence. The gentleman who was robbed asks the police officer not to hurt Oliver and follows them to the police station.

Summary: Chapter 11

The officer locks Oliver in a jail cell to await his appearance before Mr. Fang, the district magistrate. Mr. Brownlow, the gentleman, protests that he does not want to press charges. He thinks he recognizes something in Oliver's face, but cannot put his finger on it. Oliver faints in the courtroom, and Mr. Fang sentences him to three months of hard labor. The owner of the bookstall rushes in and tells Mr. Fang that two other boys committed the crime. Oliver is cleared of all charges. Pitying the sickly young Oliver, Brownlow takes him into a coach and drives away.

SUMMARY: CHAPTER 12

Oliver is delirious with a fever for days. When he awakes, Brownlow's kindly housekeeper, Mrs. Bedwin, is watching over him. He says that he feels as if his mother has come to sit by him. The story of Oliver's pitiful life brings tears to Mrs. Bedwin's eyes. Once Oliver is strong enough to sit up, Mrs. Bedwin carries him downstairs. A portrait of a young woman catches Oliver's eye and affects him greatly.

Mr. Brownlow drops in to see how Oliver is feeling. Oliver thanks him for his kindness. Brownlow exclaims with astonishment that Oliver closely resembles the young lady in the portrait. Brownlow's exclamation startles Oliver so much that the boy faints.

ANALYSIS: CHAPTERS 9–12

From today's perspective, Dickens's characterization of Fagin through Jewish stereotypes is one of the more uncomfortable aspects of *Oliver Twist*. Dickens characterizes Fagin as a "very old shrivelled Jew" with a "villainous-looking and repulsive face." Victorians stereotyped the Jews as avaricious gold worshippers, and in accordance with that stereotype, Fagin's eyes "glisten" as he takes out a "magnificent gold watch, sparkling with jewels." True to the anti-Semitic stereotype, his wealth is ill-gotten—Fagin obtains it by having others do the thieving for him, and some of those others have even been hanged for doing Fagin's bidding. Dickens's narrator continually refers to him as "the Jew" or "the old Jew," seemingly making Fagin into a representative for all Jews. When a Jewish acquaintance later took Dickens to task for his portrait of Fagin, Dickens responded that it reflected nothing other than the fact that a sizable number of the leaders of London thieving rings at the time were Jewish. Despite this answer, it is difficult to accept that his portrayal of Fagin does not involve a certain degree of bigotry.

Fagin also represents a harsh parody of the Protestant work ethic. Oliver is "anxious to be actively employed" because he notices that Fagin's "stern morality" manifests itself when Charley and the Dodger return home empty-handed. Fagin rails about the "misery of idle and lazy habits" and punishes them by denying them dinner. Victorians castigated the poor for laziness, but the work ethic they preached was in some ways responsible for creating the perversion of that ethic that Fagin represents. As a result of the "stern morality" of charitable institutions, paupers have to choose between the harsh conditions of the workhouses and the harsh conditions of the streets. Because begging is a punishable offense, those who stay outside the workhouses are often forced to turn to crime in order to survive.

Oliver's experience in the courtroom highlights the precarious position of the poor in the eyes of the law. Mr. Fang is an aptly named representative of the English legal system. The law has fangs ready to devour any unfortunate pauper brought to face "justice." Without hard evidence or witnesses, and despite Brownlow's testimony that he does not believe that Oliver is the thief, Mr. Fang convicts Oliver and sentences him to three months of hard labor. In Oliver's weakened condition, the sentence is really a sentence of death.

Oliver's inability to speak at his trial, caused by his exhaustion and sickness, metaphorically suggests the lower class's lack of political power and ability to voice its own concerns in a public forum. In 1830s England, the right to vote was based on wealth, so the poor had no say with respect to the law. Moreover, the upper classes project their own conceptions of the poor upon them—to the point of blithely redefining poor people's identities with no regard for the truth. Oliver cannot even say his name due to exhaustion and terror, so a court officer gives him the false name of "Tom White." This process of inaccurate renaming occurs throughout the hearing, as Oliver is falsely named a "young vagabond" and a "hardened scoundrel" before he is eventually falsely declared "guilty." But the name "Oliver Twist" is, in fact, no more authentic, as Mr. Bumble invents this name when Oliver is born. As these examples demonstrate, Oliver's identity has been determined by other, more powerful people throughout his life.

Oliver enters a new world when Brownlow takes him home. The English legal system and the workhouses represent a value system based on retribution, punishment, and strict morals. The Brownlow household, in contrast, operates on a basis of forgiveness and kindness. After a life of false names and false identities imposed by others, Oliver comes into contact with a portrait of a woman he closely resembles. With this event, the novel's central mystery—Oliver's true identity—is established. In contrast to the courtroom, where a multiplicity of incorrect identities are forced upon Oliver, in the Brownlow home, Oliver's resemblance to the woman's portrait suggests the elusive nature of his true identity.

CHAPTERS 13–16

SUMMARY: CHAPTER 13
Fagin erupts into a rage when the Dodger and Charley return without Oliver. Fagin tosses a pot of beer at Charley, but the pot hits Bill Sikes instead. Sikes is a rough, cruel man who makes his living by robbing houses. They resolve to find Oliver before he reveals their operation to the authorities, and persuade Nancy to go to the police station to find out what happened to him.

Nancy dresses in nice clothing, and at the police station she pretends to be Oliver's distraught sister. She learns that the gentleman from whom the handkerchief was stolen took Oliver home with him to the neighborhood of Pentonville, because the boy had fallen ill during the trial. Fagin sends Charley, Jack, and Nancy to Pentonville to find Oliver. Fagin decides to relocate his operation for the night and fills his pockets with the watches and jewelry from the hidden box after Charley, Nancy, and Jack leave.

SUMMARY: CHAPTER 14
When Oliver next enters the housekeeper's room, he notices that the portrait of the lady whom he resembles is gone. Mrs. Bedwin says that Brownlow removed it because it seemed to worry Oliver. One day, Brownlow sends for Oliver to meet him in his study. Assuming that Brownlow means to send him away, Oliver begs to remain as a servant. Brownlow assures Oliver that he wishes to be Oliver's friend. He asks Oliver to tell him his history. Before Oliver can begin, Brownlow's friend, Mr. Grimwig, arrives to visit.

Grimwig, a crotchety old man, hints that Oliver might be a boy of bad habits. Brownlow bears his friend's eccentricity with good humor. Mrs. Bedwin brings in a parcel of books delivered by the bookstall keeper's boy. Brownlow wishes to send his payment and some returns back with the boy, but he has already gone. Grimwig suggests that Brownlow send Oliver but hints that Oliver might steal the payment and the books. Wishing to prove Grimwig wrong, Brownlow sends Oliver on the errand. It grows dark and Oliver does not return.

SUMMARY: CHAPTER 15
Oliver takes a wrong turn on the way to the bookstall. Suddenly, Nancy appears. She tells everyone on the street that Oliver is her

runaway brother who joined a band of thieves, and that she is taking him back home to their parents. Everyone ignores Oliver's protests. Bill Sikes runs out of a beer shop, and he and Nancy drag
Oliver through the dark backstreets.

SUMMARY: CHAPTER 16

Nancy, Sikes, and Oliver arrive at a dilapidated house in a squalid
neighborhood. Fagin, the Dodger, and Charley laugh hysterically at
the fancy clothing Oliver is wearing. Oliver calls for help and flees,
but Sikes threatens to set his vicious dog, Bull's-eye, on him. Nancy
leaps to Oliver's defense, saying that they have ruined all his good
prospects. She has worked for Fagin since she was a small child, and
she knows that a life of disrepute lies in wait for Oliver. Fagin tries
to beat Oliver for his escape attempt, and Nancy flies at Fagin in a
rage. Sikes catches Nancy by the wrists, and she faints. They strip
Oliver of his clothing, Brownlow's money, and the books. Fagin
returns Oliver's old clothing to him and sends him to bed. Oliver had
given the clothing to Mrs. Bedwin, who sold it to a Jew, and the Jew
then delivered the clothing to Fagin and told Fagin where Oliver was.

ANALYSIS: CHAPTERS 13–16

These chapters establish a relationship between clothing and identity. The disguise that Nancy wears when she enters the police station reveals key differences between the middle and lower classes in
Victorian society. The crowning touch to her disguise is a plainly
displayed door key, which marks her as a member of a property-
owning class. Because she disguises herself as a middle-class
woman, the legal system, in the form of the police station, recognizes her as an individual worth hearing. In the attire of the middle
class, she gains both a social voice and social visibility. She becomes
an individual rather than a member of the penniless mob.

Just as Nancy assumes a middle-class identity by changing her
clothing, Oliver sheds his identity as a orphan pickpocket when he
leaves behind his pauper's clothes. Brownlow purchases an expen-
sive new suit for him. Oliver thus assumes the identity of a gentleman's son by wearing the clothing of a gentleman's son. After he
dons his new clothing, Mr. Brownlow asks him what he might like
to be when he grows up. At the workhouse, the authorities never
even bother to ask Oliver his opinion on the matter of his apprenticeship. In Victorian England, even more than today, an individ-

ual's profession determined a large part of his or her identity. The fact that no one at the workhouse asks for Oliver's opinion regarding his apprenticeship shows, once again, how much he is denied the right to define himself. Oliver's situation symbolically represents the silence of the poor. The poor cannot define their social identity—instead, the empowered classes define the identity of the poor for them. Oliver and Nancy both gain a voice the moment they shed their pauper clothing.

Class identity is correlated not only with clothing, but with history as well. Once Oliver dons his fine clothes, Brownlow asks him to give his own version of his life history. Earlier in the novel, when Oliver wears pauper's clothing, other people control his history and, therefore, his identity. When he is Sowerberry's apprentice, Oliver attempts to assume control of his identity by denying Noah's insults to his mother, but instead he receives a beating for trying to assert the correct version of his past. Once he sheds his pauper status, however, Oliver's right to explain his past is firmly established. The fact that Oliver is an orphan further underscores his lack of connection to his past. Whereas the upper classes, and particularly members of the aristocracy, are able to establish their identities by tracing their genealogies, Oliver seems to have no genealogy.

Nancy imposes another false identity on Oliver in order to kidnap him: she calls him her "dear brother." This statement is not entirely a fabrication—those who are denied families in the novel often seek out a family structure or are placed within family structures against their will. While a member of Fagin's clan, Oliver is a figurative brother to Nancy, since both are subject to the paternal authority of Fagin and are dependent upon him for their food and shelter. Through Nancy's regret at returning Oliver to Fagin, Dickens suggests that such a family, while providing companionship and a means for survival, is not ultimately nurturing or morally healthy. Nancy knows that for the rest of society, Oliver confirms the worst stereotypes of the poor as a member of Fagin's pickpocket band. Oliver's assumption of the identity of a thief comes with his assumption of the very same pauper's rags he had worn before. Donning his old clothing, the most obvious indicator of his poverty, marks him as a representative of vice for Victorian society.

Although most major characters in *Oliver Twist* are either paragons of goodness, like Oliver and Mr. Brownlow, or embodiments of evil, like Mr. Bumble, Fagin, and Sikes, Nancy's behavior spans moral extremes. Dickens's description of her manner as "remarkably free and agreeable," combined with her position as a young, unmarried female pauper, strongly implies that she is a prostitute, a profession for which Dickens's Victorian readers would have felt little sympathy. In his preface to the 1841 edition of the novel, Dickens confirms this implication, writing that "the boys are pickpockets, and the girl is a prostitute." She also spearheads the scheme to bring Oliver back into Fagin's fold. But her outburst against Sikes and Fagin for seizing and mistreating Oliver demonstrates her deep and passionate sense of morality. Most other "good" characters we meet are good because they have no firsthand experience with vice and degradation. Nancy knows degradation perfectly well, yet she is good. Her character is a forum for the novel to explore whether an individual can be redeemed from the effects of a bad environment.

At the same time, some critics have suggested that Nancy's speech, in which she announces her regret for having returned Oliver to Fagin's care, hints that the boys might also be involved in prostitution. Nancy, pointing to Oliver, declares, "I have been in the same trade, and in the same service for twelve years since." The fact that Nancy points to Oliver even as she speaks about herself implies an absolute identification between the two characters. About this detail, as about Nancy's own identity as a prostitute, the narrative is purposely vague—Victorian sensibilities mandated that explicit references to sexuality were largely avoided.

CHAPTERS 17–22

SUMMARY: CHAPTER 17

Mr. Brownlow publishes an advertisement offering a reward of five guineas for information about Oliver's whereabouts or his past. Mr. Bumble notices it in the paper while traveling to London. He quickly goes to Brownlow's home. Mr. Bumble states that, since birth, Oliver has displayed nothing but "treachery, ingratitude, and malice." Bumble tells Brownlow that Oliver attacked Noah Claypole without provocation, and Brownlow decides Oliver is nothing but an impostor. Mrs. Bedwin refuses to believe Mr. Bumble.

SUMMARY: CHAPTER 18

Fagin leaves Oliver locked up in the house for days. During the daytime, Oliver has no human company. The Dodger and Charley ask him why he does not just give himself over to Fagin, since the money comes quickly and easily in their "jolly life." Fagin gradually allows Oliver to spend more time in the other boys' company. Sometimes, Fagin himself regales his crew with funny stories of robberies he committed in his youth. Oliver often laughs at the stories despite himself. Fagin's plan has been to isolate Oliver until he comes to be so grateful for any human contact that he will do whatever Fagin asks.

SUMMARY: CHAPTER 19

Sikes plans to rob a house, but he needs a small boy for the job. Fagin offers Oliver's services. Sikes warns Oliver that he will kill him if he shows any signs of hesitation during the robbery. Sikes arranges to have Nancy deliver Oliver to the scene. Fagin watches Nancy for any signs of hesitation. Despite her earlier protests against trapping Oliver in a life of crime, she betrays no further misgivings.

SUMMARY: CHAPTER 20

Fagin informs Oliver that he will be taken to Sikes's residence that night. He gives Oliver a book to read. Oliver waits, shivering in horror at the book's bloody tales of famous criminals and murderers. Nancy arrives to take him away. Oliver considers calling for help on the streets. Reading his thoughts on his face, Nancy warns him that he could get both of them into deep trouble. They arrive at Sikes's residence, and Sikes shows Oliver a pistol. He warns Oliver that if he causes any trouble, he will kill him. At five in the morning, they prepare to leave for the job.

SUMMARY: CHAPTER 21

Sikes takes Oliver on a long journey to the town of Shepperton. They arrive after dark.

SUMMARY: CHAPTER 22

Sikes leads Oliver to a ruinous house where his partners in crime, Toby Crackit and Barney, are waiting. At half past one, Sikes and Crackit set out with Oliver. They arrive at the targeted house and climb over the wall surrounding it. Only then does Oliver realize that he will be made to participate in a robbery. Horrified, he begs Sikes to let him go. Sikes curses and prepares to shoot him, but Crackit knocks the pistol away, saying that gunfire will draw attention.

Crackit clasps his hand over Oliver's mouth while Sikes pries open a tiny window. Sikes instructs Oliver to enter through the window and open the street door to let them inside, reminding him that he is within shooting range all the while. Oliver plans to dash for the stairs and warn the family. Sikes lowers him through the window. However, the residents of the house awake, and one shoots Oliver's arm. Sikes pulls Oliver back through the window. He and Crackit flee with the bleeding Oliver.

ANALYSIS: CHAPTERS 17–22

Oliver's domestic relationship with Fagin and his gang contributes to the novel's argument that that the environment in which one is raised is a greater determining factor on one's character than biological nature. The need for companionship, Dickens suggests, drives people to accept whichever community accepts them in return. As Oliver begins to find humor and joy in the companionship of the thieves, it becomes evident how easy it is for Fagin to corrupt Oliver. With the institution of the oppressive Poor Laws, it is no wonder that penniless, friendless children will adopt as family any person who is generous to them and will readily adopt that person's values. The Artful Dodger and Charley Bates are, aside from their crimes, quite likeable characters. As his name implies, the Dodger is highly intelligent, and Charley is given to bursts of uncontrollable laughter at little provocation. Both, one imagines, could have thrived in legitimate society, were that society willing to admit them to its ranks.

The fact that Oliver speaks and carries himself with a demeanor that is much more sophisticated than that of the rest of Fagin's boys suggests that Dickens is using Oliver to show that even when people are born into squalid conditions, they can appreciate goodness and morality. When the Dodger and Charley pick Brownlow's pocket, and again when Sikes and Crackit order Oliver into the house, Oliver reacts with shock and horror at the idea of stealing. It is unclear where he has acquired such moral fastidiousness. He could not have learned it amid the life or death struggles of the workhouse. The Dodger and Charley speak in the slang of street children, using expressions like "scragged," "rum dog," "peaching," and "fogles and tickers." But Oliver does not understand what such expressions mean. He himself speaks in proper King's English: "I would rather go," "you're one, are you not?" Because even Mr. Bumble speaks with a comical vulgar accent, Oliver could not have picked up his refined speech patterns from him. It seems that Oliver's careful speech is a symptom of his innate moral goodness.

Yet the suggestion that Oliver is innately good complicates Dickens's argument that corruption is bred by the horrible living conditions of the lower classes, rather than inherently born into their characters. Descriptions of Oliver's face, in fact, seem to suggest that morality can be born into character. Mr. Sowerberry enlists Oliver to serve in funerals on account of the "expression of melancholy in his face." The usually unperceptive Toby Crackit notes that Oliver's "mug is a fortun' to him," meaning that his innocent-looking face is worth money to the thieves. Mr. Brownlow sees clearly the resemblance between Oliver and the woman in the portrait, thus providing both himself and us with the first hint that the workhouse-born Oliver has an identity that is worth discovering. Dickens clearly protests against the idea propounded by Mr. Bumble, that the poor are born with an affinity for vice and crime. Yet it sometimes seems as if Oliver has been born with an affinity for virtue and love, just as he was born with his angelic face.

But even Oliver's captivating face does not give him immunity against irrational malice, embodied by characters such as Bumble. Bumble names Oliver as a child born of "low and vicious" parents, reproducing the stereotype that the poor inherit a criminal nature. Moreover, Bumble narrates the incident of Oliver's attack on Noah Claypole in the same light. Oliver was "low and vicious" for trying to define his identity on his own terms. Mr. Bumble shows Brownlow his own identification papers to prove his statement. His status as the middle-class beadle for a workhouse gives him the right to speak for Oliver and therefore to define Oliver's identity as he sees fit. With his identification papers, Bumble has the power of the state to back up his word. Oliver only has his own word to back him up. Outside of the workhouse, Oliver has no legal existence unless he commits a crime and enters the courtroom. The poor are thus reduced to a public existence as criminals, corpses, and "idle, lazy" paupers living on state charity. The state chooses to recognize their existence only when they commit crimes, die, or enter the workhouses.

CHAPTERS 23–28

SUMMARY: CHAPTER 23

Mr. Bumble visits Mrs. Corney, the widowed matron of the workhouse, to deliver some wine. Mrs. Corney offers him tea. Mr. Bumble slowly moves his chair closer to Mrs. Corney's and kisses her on the lips. An old pauper woman interrupts them to report that Old Sally, a woman under Mrs. Corney's care, is close to death and wishes to tell Mrs. Corney something. Irritated, Mrs. Corney leaves. Alone in Mrs. Corney's room, Mr. Bumble takes "an exact inventory of the furniture."

SUMMARY: CHAPTER 24

Mrs. Corney enters Old Sally's room. The dying woman awakens and asks that her other bedside companions be sent away. She then confesses that she once robbed a woman in her care. The woman had been found pregnant on the road, and Sally had attended the childbirth. The woman had given Sally a gold locket, saying it might lead to people who would care for the child. The child's name was Oliver. Sally dies, and Mrs. Corney leaves. She tells the nurses who attended Sally that Sally had nothing to say after all.

SUMMARY: CHAPTER 25

Crackit arrives at Fagin's. Fagin has learned from the newspapers that the robbery has failed. Crackit informs Fagin that Oliver has been shot and claims that the entire population of the area then came after them. Crackit says that he and Sikes fled, leaving Oliver in a ditch.

SUMMARY: CHAPTER 26

Fagin rushes into a pub called the Three Cripples to look for a man named Monks. Not finding him, he hurries to Sikes's residence. At Sikes's residence, he finds Nancy, who, in a drunken stupor, reports that Sikes is hiding. Fagin relates Oliver's misfortune, and Nancy cries that she hopes Oliver is dead, because she believes that living with Fagin is worse than death. Fagin replies that Oliver is worth hundreds of pounds to him. He returns to his house to find Monks waiting for him. Monks asks why Fagin has chosen to send Oliver out on such a mission rather than make the boy into a simple pickpocket. It becomes clear that Monks has some interest in Oliver. Monks was looking for Oliver and saw him the day Oliver was arrested. Moreover, Fagin notes that Monks wants Oliver to be made into a hardened thief. Monks becomes alarmed, thinking he sees the shadow of a woman. The two stop talking and leave Fagin's house.

SUMMARY: CHAPTER 27

Mrs. Corney, flustered, returns to her room. She and Mr. Bumble drink spiked peppermint together. They flirt and kiss. Bumble mentions that the current master of the workhouse is on his deathbed. He hints that he could fill the vacancy and marry Mrs. Corney. She blushes and consents. Bumble travels to inform Sowerberry that his services will be needed for Old Sally. Bumble happens upon Charlotte feeding Noah Claypole oysters in the kitchen. When Noah tells Charlotte he wants to kiss her, Bumble lectures them for their immoral ways.

SUMMARY: CHAPTER 28

The night after the failed robbery, Oliver awakens delirious. He gets up and stumbles over to the same house Sikes tried to get him to rob. Inside, Mr. Giles and Mr. Brittles, two servants, regale the other servants with the details of the night's events, presenting themselves as intrepid heroes. Oliver's feeble knock at the door frightens everyone. Brittles opens the door to find Oliver lying on the stoop. They exclaim that Oliver is one of the thieves and drag him inside. The niece of the wealthy mistress of the mansion calls downstairs to ask if the poor creature is badly wounded. She sends Brittles to fetch a doctor and constable while Giles gently carries Oliver upstairs.

ANALYSIS: CHAPTERS 23–28

By contrasting two kinds of theft, Dickens shows how his culture is quick to condemn more obvious acts of theft, but ignores theft that occurs in more subtle ways. After presenting Sikes and Crackit's botched attempt at theft, the novel quickly shifts to the scene of a very different form of thievery. Mrs. Corney, the middle-class matron of the workhouse, enjoys far more luxury than the pauper residents. They are crammed into tiny, unheated spaces, while Mrs. Corney enjoys a room to herself with a blazing fire during the bitterly cold winter. The amenities of her apartment, which draw Mr. Bumble's eyes and heart in her direction, represent money that would have been more justly spent on the paupers under her care. Thus, her lifestyle is based on theft, but, because she is robbing those who have nothing, her theft will never be acknowledged.

The description of Mrs. Corney implies that the middle class controls conceptions of what is right and wrong, since church officials, intellectuals, and public officers—who have the authority to declare what is right and wrong—are all part of the middle class. With this control, they are able to ignore their own version of thievery—subtly shortchanging the lower classes—and at the same time condemn the lower-class version of thievery—stealing physical objects from the rich. The middle class's sense of entitlement and belief that the poor are inherently morally wretched allow its members to easily rationalize the many ways in which they make sure the poor remain so.

Dickens uses an ironic dialogue between Mrs. Corney and Mr. Bumble to demonstrate their hypocrisy. Mr. Bumble remarks that Mrs. Corney's cat and kittens receive better treatment than the workhouse paupers. The cats bask in front of a blazing fire while the paupers freeze in inadequately heated dormitories. Mr. Bumble remarks that he would drown any cat that was not grateful to live with Mrs. Corney. Mrs. Corney calls him a cruel man for saying that he would drown a cat. Mrs. Corney, of course, ignores her own great cruelty to the paupers, yet bristles at the implication of a drowned cat. By treating the paupers worse than animals, these so-called charitable officials violate their basic rights as human beings.

Mr. Bumble's proposal to Mrs. Corney is a parody of a certain kind of middle-class marriage. Mr. Bumble whispers sweet nothings to Mrs. Corney, but for all of his romantic pretensions, his proposal is really inspired by Mrs. Corney's material wealth. When she leaves the room, he verifies that her dishware is made from silver and that her clothing is of "good fashion and texture." He assesses the exact condition of her furniture and ascertains that her small padlocked box contains money. At the end of this extensive inventory, he decides to go through with his proposal. During the Victorian era, many marriages were primarily economic arrangements, especially for people of middle-class status and above. Dickens, however, was a die-hard romantic. In *Oliver Twist*, he champions the romantic concept of marriage based on love. This idea will become increasingly important during the latter half of the novel.

With the introduction of Monks, the novel begins to take on the clear attributes of a detective story, especially because we are unsure of who the man is and why he might be interested in Oliver. Even Dickens's description of Monks as "a dark figure" who lurks "in deep shadow" is mysterious. Furthermore, the chapter implies that Monks will be involved in the protracted unveiling of Oliver's identity, and, after Monks's conversation with Fagin, our curiosity seeks satisfaction from the lingering bewilderment. Monks's claim that he saw "the shadow of a woman . . . pass[ing] along the wainscot like a breath" introduces a note of suspense and even of the supernatural, which grows more pronounced as the story continues.

CHAPTERS 29–32

SUMMARY: CHAPTER 29

The chapter begins with a description of Mrs. Maylie, the mistress of the house at which Oliver is shot. She is a kindly, old-fashioned elderly woman. Her niece, Miss Rose, is an angelic beauty of seventeen. Mr. Losberne, the eccentric local bachelor surgeon, arrives in a fluster, stating his wonderment at the fact that neither woman is dead of fright at having a burglar in their house. He proceeds to attend to Oliver for a long while. When he returns, he asks the women if they have actually seen the thief. They have not, and, since Giles has enjoyed the commendations for his bravery, he has not told the women that the thief he shot is a small boy. The ladies accompany the surgeon to see the culprit for the first time.

SUMMARY: CHAPTER 30

Upon seeing Oliver, Miss Rose exclaims that he cannot possibly be a burglar unless older, evil men have forced him into the trade. She begs her aunt not to send the child to prison. Mrs. Maylie replies that she intends to send him to prison nonetheless. They wait all day for Oliver to awake in order to determine whether he is a bad child or not. Oliver relates his life history to them that evening, bringing tears to the eyes of his audience. Mr. Losberne hurries downstairs and asks if Giles and Brittles can swear before the constable that Oliver is the same boy they saw in the house the night before. Meanwhile, police officers from London, summoned by Brittles and Giles that morning, arrive to assess the situation.

SUMMARY: CHAPTER 31

Duff and Blathers, the officers, examine the crime scene, while the surgeon and the women try to think of a way to conceal Oliver's part in the crime. The officers determine that two men and a boy were involved, judging from the footprints and the size of the window. Mr. Losberne tells them that Giles merely mistook Oliver for the guilty party. He tells them that Oliver was wounded accidentally by a spring-gun while trespassing on a neighbor's property. Giles and Brittles state that they cannot swear that he is the boy they saw that night. The officers depart and the matter is settled without incident.

SUMMARY: CHAPTER 32

> *Who can tell how scenes of peace and quietude sink into the minds of pain-worn dwellers in close and noisy places, and carry their own freshness deep into their jaded hearts!* (See QUOTATIONS, p. 32)

Over a period of weeks, Oliver slowly begins to recover. He begs for some way to repay his benefactors' kindness. They tell him he can do so after he recovers his health. He laments not being able to tell Brownlow and Mrs. Bedwin what has happened to him. Mr. Losberne takes Oliver to London to see them. To Oliver's bitter disappointment, he and Losberne discover that Brownlow, Mrs. Bedwin, and Mr. Grimwig have moved to the West Indies. Mrs. Maylie and Miss Rose then take him to the countryside. In the blissful rural environment, Oliver's health improves vastly, as do his reading and writing skills. He and the ladies become greatly attached to each other during the months they spend there.

ANALYSIS: CHAPTERS 29–32

Through Rose's reaction to Oliver, Dickens presents delinquency as a problem determined by culture rather than by innate character. Upon seeing Oliver, Rose imagines his entire history at a glance. Unlike most adults who have tried to second-guess him, Rose's hypotheses about his past and personality are accurate. She surmises that Oliver took part in the attempted burglary because he has never "known a mother's love" or because he suffered "illusage and blows" and "the want of bread." She names all the miserable conditions of poverty that may have "driven him to herd with men who have forced him to guilt." Like Brownlow, and unlike the English legal system, the Maylies believe in forgiveness and kindness. Dickens uses these characters, who believe that Oliver is innately good but born into a bad environment, to show that vices can be combated by improving the material conditions of the poor rather than by punishing them. The Maylies recognize that Oliver's surroundings have determined his behavior but not necessarily his nature, and, as a result, for the first time in his life Oliver is given the chance to narrate his life history on his own terms. This event is an important step in establishing his identity as separate from his surroundings.

The Maylie household in effect simulates a benevolent courtroom, giving Oliver a voice and actually listening to that voice. In this capacity, the courtroom of the Maylie household is wholly different from the typical courtroom of the English legal system. In the courtroom of Mr. Fang, which Dickens depicts in the novel, Oliver is not permitted to testify on his own behalf. Moreover, even in the absence of conclusive evidence, the magistrate still convicts him of the crime of pickpocketing. In the courtroom of the Maylie household, Oliver not only testifies for himself, but he also admits his part in the attempted burglary. However, rather than convict him, his testimony exonerates him, since the Maylies are more concerned with the fact that Oliver can be saved from committing further crimes than with punishing him for the crime that he committed. For the Maylies, Oliver's entire history and personality matter more than any single action of his.

Losberne's conversation with Giles and Brittles elaborates the two kinds of moral authority by which characters can be judged in *Oliver Twist*: the moral authority of the English court system and the higher spiritual authority of God. Losberne appeals to Giles's fear of God's higher authority to keep him from telling the constable that Oliver took part in the attempted burglary. His question to Giles and Brittles—"Are you, on your solemn oaths, able to identify that boy?"—asks them if they are morally able to identify Oliver to the law and live with the consequences. Losberne implies that Giles will be responsible for Oliver's death if Giles's statement sends him to the English courtroom, since the harsh, literal-minded authority of the English legal system would sentence Oliver to death for participating in a burglary. But the novel suggests that the higher, spiritual authority of God would sentence Giles to hell for complicity in the death of a child. Even though Giles, Brittles, and Losberne are all certain that it was indeed Oliver who committed the crime, the three men are in a position to exercise mercy, while the court system is not. The scene suggests that mercy is frequently more valuable than justice, especially when crimes or sins are committed within extenuating circumstances.

The maternal roles that Mrs. Maylie and Rose play in Oliver's life place Oliver in a normal family structure for the first time in the novel, and Dickens's characterization of the upper-class family complicates his original intention of giving voice to the poor. Oliver is the object of women's kindness when both Mrs. Bedwin and Nancy step in to offer him some measure of maternal protection. But unlike Mrs. Bedwin and Nancy, the Maylie women are upper-class, and Dickens's portrayal of them reveals an implicit bias toward the upper class that complicates his explicit attempts to speak for the poor. Blessed with the freedom and leisure to do nothing all day but read, pick flowers, take walks, and play the piano, the Maylies lead lives of perfect bliss, in which Oliver is thrilled to take part. Dickens condemns the money-grubbing tendencies of characters like Fagin and Mr. Bumble, but his idyllic portrait of the moneyed life almost makes Fagin's and Bumble's avarice seem more understandable.

The idyll of Oliver's life with the Maylies is also related to their move to the countryside, and Dickens suggests that rural life is superior in all ways to city life. In the country, even poor people have "clean houses," and woodland "scenes of peace and quietude" are described as sufficient comfort even for those who lead "lives of toil." Dickens's portrait of rural poverty as perfectly pleasant cannot be entirely accurate, in light of the vast numbers of peasants who chose to migrate to the city in his time. His description of the countryside as a site of class harmony may be a result of Oliver's sudden migration into the ranks of the upper class as much as anything else. We already know that the condition of the poor in cities is horrific, and the extravagant lives of the wealthy people who live alongside them may look grotesque and downright immoral in contrast. But if the rural poor lead comfortable lives, there is no call to condemn the leisurely existence of the wealthy Maylies.

CHAPTERS 33–37

SUMMARY: CHAPTER 33

Without warning, Rose falls ill with a serious fever. Mrs. Maylie sends Oliver to mail a letter requesting Losberne's assistance. On his return journey, Oliver stumbles against a tall man wrapped in a cloak. The man curses Oliver, asks what he is doing there, and then falls violently to the ground, "writhing and foaming." Oliver secures help for the man before he returns home and forgets the incident entirely. Rose's condition declines rapidly. Losberne arrives and examines her. He states there is little hope for her recovery. However, Rose soon draws back from the brink of death and begins to improve.

SUMMARY: CHAPTER 34

Giles and Harry Maylie, Mrs. Maylie's son, arrive to see Rose. Harry is angry that his mother has not written him sooner. Mrs. Maylie replies that Rose needs long-lasting love rather than the whims of a youthful suitor. Mrs. Maylie tells her son that he must consider the public opinion in his desire to marry Rose for love. She mentions a "stain" on Rose's name: although Rose herself has never committed any crime, public opinion may well convict her for the misdeeds of her parents. Mrs. Maylie hints that Rose's social status may thwart Harry's ambitions to run for Parliament and that those thwarted ambitions might eventually destroy his love for Rose. In the short run, Mrs. Maylie says, he must choose between his prospects for material gain and his love for Rose. In the long run, however, there is no choice at all, in Mrs. Maylie's opinion: the negative judgment of society is powerful enough to defeat love. Harry declares that his love for Rose is solid and lasting. While Rose recovers, Oliver and Harry collect flowers for her room. One day Oliver falls asleep while reading by a window. He has a nightmare that Fagin and a man are pointing at him and whispering. Fagin says, "It is he, sure enough!" Oliver awakes to see Fagin and the stranger he saw when he mailed the letter peering through the window. They disappear rapidly as Oliver calls for help.

SUMMARY: CHAPTER 35

Harry and Giles rush to Oliver's aid. Upon hearing about Fagin and the man, they search the fields around the house but find no trace of them. They circulate a description of Fagin but find no clues to his whereabouts. Harry declares his love to Rose. Although she returns his love, she says she cannot marry him owing to the circumstances of her birth. His station is much higher than hers, and she does not want to hinder his ambitions. Harry states that he plans to propose marriage one more time, but that, if she again refuses, he will not mention it again.

SUMMARY: CHAPTER 36

Before Harry and Losberne depart, Harry asks that Oliver secretly write him a letter every two weeks, telling him everything Oliver and the ladies do and say. From a window, Rose tearfully watches the coach carry Harry and Losberne away.

SUMMARY: CHAPTER 37

The narrator tells us that Mr. Bumble has married Mrs. Corney and become the master of the workhouse. He regrets giving up his position as beadle, but regrets giving up his bachelorhood even more. After a morning of bickering with his wife, he stops in a pub for a drink. A man in a dark cape is sitting there, and he recognizes Mr. Bumble as the former beadle. He offers Mr. Bumble money for information about Old Sally, the woman who attended Oliver's birth. Mr. Bumble informs him that Old Sally is dead but mentions that he knows a woman who spoke to the old woman on her deathbed. The stranger asks that Mr. Bumble bring this woman to see him the following evening. He gives his name as Monks.

ANALYSIS: CHAPTERS 33–37

The relationship between Harry and Rose illustrates that although marriage based on love is difficult, Dickens values it more highly than marriage based on social station. However, Rose and Mrs. Maylie both believe that marriage based on love is problematic. Rose refuses to marry Harry for the same reasons that Mrs. Maylie says she should not. Rose calls herself "a friendless, portionless girl" with a "blight" upon her name. As a penniless, nameless girl, she says to Harry that his friends will suspect that she "sordidly yielded to your first passion and fastened myself . . . on all your hopes and projects." In other words, she fears that outsiders will believe that she slept with Harry outside of wedlock and secured his hand in marriage in that way. Thus, she demonstrates her awareness of the tendency of "respectable" society to assume the worst about individuals of low social standing, a tendency that has almost ruined Oliver's life time and again.

Rose's fear that others would find her marriage to Harry "sordid" reveals the fundamental irrationality of the society whose opinion she fears. Victorians who belonged to the middle and upper classes often married for economic reasons. Individuals usually married someone from a similar economic and social class because, presumably, marrying down would harm their social and economic interests. Logically, we might assume that a marriage between two people of different classes was more, not less, likely to be based on love and higher spiritual values, since it would violate the material interests of at least one party. Yet Rose predicts that others would attribute her marriage to Harry to factors far less honorable than love. Society's inclination to assume the worst about those of low social standing is so strong that it can lead to patently irrational conclusions.

Rose regrets that she cannot offer Harry an economically profitable and socially acceptable marriage, but Dickens criticizes socially or economically motivated marriage. Mr. Bumble and Mrs. Corney demonstrate one such marriage, and the Bumbles lead a miserable life. They dislike each other intensely. Mr. Bumble regrets marrying for "six teaspoons, a pair of sugar-tongs, and a milk-pot; with a small quantity of second-hand furniture, and twenty pound in money." He bases his marriage on class similarities and not on personal compatibility, and the result is a complete disaster.

Like Nancy and Oliver, Bumble learns of the influence that clothing exercises upon identity. Bumble has given up his position as the parish beadle to become the workhouse master. Having exchanged one identity for another, he now regrets the change. After leaving his position as beadle, he realizes how important the beadle's clothing was to the position. Dickens writes, "Strip the bishop of his apron, or the beadle of his hat and lace; what are they? Men. Mere men. Dignity, and even holiness too, sometimes, are more questions of coat and waistcoat than some people imagine." The power and dignity of privileged roles are not qualities inherent in the men who occupy them. They are, like clothing, merely purchased and worn, and they can be taken off as easily as they were put on.

CHAPTERS 38–41

SUMMARY: CHAPTER 38

During a storm, Mr. and Mrs. Bumble travel to a sordid section of town near a swollen river to meet Monks in a decaying building. While Mr. Bumble shivers in fear, Mrs. Bumble coolly bargains with Monks. They settle on a price of twenty-five pounds for her information. Mrs. Bumble relates how Old Sally robbed Oliver's mother. Mrs. Bumble says she discovered a ragged pawnbroker's receipt in Old Sally's dead hands and that she redeemed it for the gold locket, which she then hands to Monks. Inside, he finds a wedding ring and two locks of hair. The name "Agnes" is engraved on the ring, along with a blank for the surname. Monks ties the locket to a weight and drops it into the river.

SUMMARY & ANALYSIS

SUMMARY: CHAPTER 39

Bill Sikes is ill with a fever. Nancy nurses him anxiously, despite his surly attitude. Fagin and his friends drop in to deliver wine and food. Sikes demands that Fagin give him money. Nancy and Fagin travel to Fagin's haunt. He is about to delve into his store of cash when Monks arrives and asks to speak to Fagin alone. The two men leave for a secluded room, but Nancy follows them and eavesdrops. The narrator does not reveal the content of the conversation. After Monks departs, Fagin gives Nancy the money. Perturbed by what she has heard, she dashes into the streets and away from Sikes's residence before returning to deliver the money. Sikes does not notice her nervousness until a few days later. Sensing something, he demands that she sit by him. After he falls asleep, she hurries to a hotel in a wealthy area. She begs the servants to allow her to speak to Miss Maylie, who is staying there. Disapprovingly, they conduct her upstairs.

SUMMARY: CHAPTER 40

> *Pity us, lady—pity us for having only one feeling of*
> *the woman left and for having that turned . . . from a*
> *comfort and a pride into a new means of violence*
> *and suffering.* (See QUOTATIONS, p. 64)

Nancy confesses to Rose that she is the one who kidnapped Oliver on his errand for Mr. Brownlow. She relates that she overheard Monks tell Fagin that he is Oliver's brother. Monks wants Oliver's identity to remain unknown so that Monks himself can claim their family's full inheritance. Monks would kill Oliver if he could do so without endangering himself. He has also promised to pay Fagin if Oliver is recaptured. Rose offers to help Nancy leave her life of crime. Nancy replies that she cannot, because she is attached to Sikes despite his abusive ways. She refuses Rose's money. Before leaving, Nancy informs Rose that she can be found on London Bridge between eleven and twelve every Sunday night in case further testimony is needed.

SUMMARY: CHAPTER 41

Not long after Nancy and Rose's meeting, Oliver tells Rose that he saw Mr. Brownlow on the street. Oliver and Mr. Giles have ascertained Brownlow's address, so Rose immediately takes Oliver there. Mr. Grimwig is visiting when they arrive. Rose tells Brownlow that Oliver wants to thank him. Once Rose and Brownlow are alone, she relates Nancy's story. Oliver is brought in to see Brownlow and Mrs. Bedwin. After their happy reunion, Brownlow and Rose relay Nancy's information to Mrs. Maylie and Losberne. Brownlow asks if he can include Grimwig in the matter, and Losberne insists that they include Harry. They agree to keep everything a secret from Oliver and decide to contact Nancy the following Sunday on London Bridge.

ANALYSIS: CHAPTERS 38–41

The title of *Oliver Twist* is deceptively simple. Although it does nothing more than state the protagonist's name, the central mystery of the novel is, in fact, the protagonist's true identity. Oliver's misfortunes have had much to do with the false or mistaken identities others have thrust upon him. Dickens conceals the solution to the mystery of his true identity, leaving just a clue here and there in order to move the plot forward. Various people seek to conceal Oliver's identity for their own personal gain. Oliver's identity is intertwined with Monks's identity, and the connection between the two of them has shrouded both their identities in mystery. Once it becomes clear that Oliver and Monks are brothers, the novel enters its final stage. We begin to have some idea of who Oliver might be, but the story continues since Oliver himself has yet to find out.

The meeting of Nancy and Rose represents the clash of two very different worlds. Rose has been raised amid love and plenty, and, as a result, her virtue and kindness are almost unreal. On the other hand, Nancy has struggled for survival in the streets, and instead of conventional virtue, her life is full of crime and violence. Yet both were once penniless, nameless orphans. Rose simply had the good luck to be taken in by Mrs. Maylie, who offered her a road of escape from her unfortunate position. Now, Rose offers Nancy a similar road of escape, but it is already too late for Nancy. Their characters can be seen as part of Dickens's argument that the environment in which people are raised and the company that they keep have a greater influence on their quality of character than any inborn traits. Rose and Nancy were born in similar circumstances: only the environment in which each was raised has made them so different.

Nancy's decision to confront Rose with information about Oliver stands in opposition to her earlier decision to drag Oliver back to Fagin. Just as Nancy causes Oliver to become a thief earlier in the novel by sending him to Fagin, her decision to reveal the information she holds regarding his inheritance may cause him to become wealthy. Furthermore, Nancy's honorable act directly contradicts Victorian stereotypes of the poor as fundamentally immoral and ignoble. It demonstrates that there are different levels of vice and that an individual who partakes of one level does not necessarily partake of the others. Nancy has been a thief since childhood, she drinks to excess, and she is a prostitute. Despite these tainting circumstances, however, she is incredibly virtuous where the most important matters, those of life and death, are concerned. With her character, Dickens suggests that the violation of property laws and sexual mores is not incompatible with deep generosity and morality.

In many ways, Nancy, the paragon of vice, appears here as more virtuous than Rose, the paragon of virtue. Rose stands to lose nothing by helping Oliver, but Nancy could lose her life. Fagin's central threat to keep his associates from acting against his interests is the threat of legal "justice." He knows in intimate detail the criminal activities of everyone in his social circle. Fagin can send Nancy to the gallows for talking to anyone outside his circle of criminal associates.

Nancy regrets her life of vice, but she refuses Rose's offer to help her change it. Nancy sees herself, as Rose puts it, as "a woman lost almost beyond redemption." It seems as if she herself assimilates to the judgments that intolerant characters like Mr. Bumble have passed upon her. Yet Nancy's love for Sikes is more crucial to her decision to return to her old life than any belief that she has strayed too far from the path of moral goodness. The different light in which society treats Nancy's and Rose's romantic attachments reveals the extent of its prejudices against the poor. It is considered a virtue when a woman like Rose is unconditionally faithful to a respectable young man like Harry Maylie. Yet when a woman like Nancy displays the same fidelity to a dreadful fellow like Sikes, it becomes "a new means of violence and suffering." This contrast demonstrates that socioeconomic status has the power to color all aspects of an individual's life, even the private emotions of love and sentiment.

CHAPTERS 42–48

SUMMARY: CHAPTER 42
Noah Claypole and Charlotte flee to London after robbing Mr. Sowerberry. They stop at the Three Cripples inn, where they meet Fagin and Barney. Fagin invites Noah to join his gang, assigning him to rob children.

SUMMARY: CHAPTER 43
Noah meets Fagin at his home. The Artful Dodger has been arrested for stealing a handkerchief. Noah's first job is to go to the police station to watch the Dodger's trial. The Dodger, joking all the while, is convicted and sentenced to transportation. Noah hurries back to tell Fagin.

SUMMARY: CHAPTER 44
Fagin is visiting Sikes when Nancy tries to leave for London Bridge at eleven on Sunday. Sikes drags her into another room and restrains her for an hour. When he departs, Fagin asks that Nancy conduct him downstairs. He whispers to her that he will help her leave the brute Sikes if she wants. Fagin imagines that Nancy has wanted to meet a new lover that night. He hopes to persuade her to murder Sikes and bring her new love into his gang, so he can solidify his control over her. He plans to watch her in order to discover the identity of her new love, hoping to blackmail her with this information.

SUMMARY: CHAPTER 45
Fagin tells Noah that he will pay him a pound to follow Nancy. The following Sunday, when Sikes is away, he takes Noah to Sikes's residence. At eleven, Nancy leaves the apartment. Noah follows at a discreet distance.

SUMMARY: CHAPTER 46
Nancy meets Mr. Brownlow and Rose on London Bridge and leads them to a secluded spot. Noah hears Nancy beg them to ensure that none of her associates get into trouble because of her choice to help Oliver. They agree, and Nancy tells them when they will most likely see Monks visiting the public house. They hope to catch Monks and force the truth about Oliver from him. Nancy's description of Monks startles Mr. Brownlow, who appears to know him. Brown-

low begs Nancy to accept their help, but she says that she is chained to her life. He and Rose depart. Nancy cries violently and then heads for home. Noah hurries to Fagin's house.

SUMMARY: CHAPTER 47

When Sikes delivers stolen goods to Fagin that night, Fagin and Noah relate the details of Nancy's trip. Fagin does not tell Sikes that Nancy insisted that her associates not get into trouble. In a rage, Sikes rushes home and beats Nancy to death while she begs for mercy.

SUMMARY: CHAPTER 48

> *He threw himself upon the road—on his back upon the road. At his head it stood, silent, erect, and still—a living grave-stone, with its epitaph in blood.*
> (See QUOTATIONS, p. 65)

In the morning, Sikes flees London, seeing suspicious looks everywhere. He stops at a country inn to eat. Seeing a bloodstain on Sikes's hat, a salesman grabs it to demonstrate the quality of his stain remover. Sikes flees the inn. He overhears some men talking about the murder at the post office. He wanders the road, haunted by the image of Nancy's dead eyes. A local barn catches fire, and Sikes helps put out the fire. Sikes decides to return to London and hide. Afraid that his dog, Bull's-eye, will give him away, he tries to drown the animal, but it escapes.

ANALYSIS: CHAPTERS 42–48

Although Fagin claims to be in partnership with his associates, protecting them in exchange for their loyalty, in the end, he manipulates them so that his own self-interest is better served. He watches the people around him with special care and translates his knowledge about them into power. A prime example of this strategy is his hope to use Nancy's possible lover to control her through blackmail. Even worse, he reveals Nancy's betrayal of the band's code of silence to Sikes in the worst, most treacherous light possible. He describes her actions in such a way as to inspire Sikes's murderous rage. Having Nancy killed is at least as beneficial to Fagin as to Sikes, but Fagin is unwilling to risk doing the deed himself. Instead, he uses his knowledge about Nancy and about Sikes's character to manipulate Sikes into committing the horrible crime.

Oliver Twist explores different varieties of justice—that served by the English court system; spiritual or godly justice; and, with Sikes's crime, personal justice, or the torments of conscience. Justice for Sikes's "foulest and most cruel" of crimes is served almost instantly, as Sikes's guilt immediately subjects him to horrific mental torture. The passages exploring his mental state are among the most psychologically intricate in the novel. Sikes cannot cleanse himself of Nancy's blood, either figuratively or literally. Visions of Nancy's dead eyes disturb him greatly, and he fears being seen. During his desperate flight from London, he feels as though everyone is watching suspiciously. Sikes's remorse and paranoia shape and twist the world around him. The traveling salesman who claims to offer "the infallible and invaluable composition for removing all sorts of stain," including bloodstains, is so canny in his offer to help Sikes remove his stains that the salesman could almost be a figment of Sikes's haunted imagination. Likewise, the burning barn, which essentially serves no purpose in the plot, seems to be a herald of the fires of hell Sikes sees in his future.

Unlike Oliver, who spends much of the novel trying to discover his identity, Sikes desperately wishes to hide his identity. However, his dog, Bull's-eye, acts as a kind of walking name tag. The animal follows him everywhere. Indeed, Sikes's animal even leaves his mark at the scene of the crime—his bloodstained footprints cover the room where Nancy is killed. Bull's-eye often functions as an alter ego for Sikes: the animal is vicious and brutal, just like its owner. Sikes's desire to kill the dog symbolically and psychologically represents a desire to kill himself, the murderer he has become.

CHAPTERS 49–53

SUMMARY: CHAPTER 49

Mr. Brownlow has captured Monks and brought him to the Brownlow home. Monks's real name is Edward Leeford. Brownlow was a good friend of Monks's father, Mr. Leeford. Mr. Leeford was a young man when his family forced him to marry a wealthy older woman. The couple eventually separated but did not divorce, and Edward and his mother went to Paris. Meanwhile, Mr. Leeford fell in love with Agnes Fleming, a retired naval officer's daughter, who became pregnant with Oliver. The relative who had benefited most from Mr. Leeford's forced marriage repented and left Mr. Leeford a

fortune. Mr. Leeford left a portrait of his beloved Agnes in Brownlow's care while he went to Rome to claim his inheritance. Mr. Leeford's wife, hearing of his good fortune, traveled with Edward to
meet him there. However, in Rome, Mr. Leeford took ill and died.
Brownlow reports that he knows that Monks's mother burned Mr.
Leeford's will, so Mr. Leeford's newfound fortune fell to his wife and
son. After his mother died, Monks lived in the West Indies on their
ill-gotten fortune. Brownlow, remembering Oliver's resemblance to
the woman in the portrait, had gone there to find Monks after Oliver
was kidnapped. Meanwhile, the search for Sikes continues.

Summary: Chapter 50

Toby Crackit and Tom Chitling flee to a squalid island after Fagin
and Noah are captured by the authorities. Sikes's dog shows up at
the house that serves as their hiding place. Sikes arrives soon after.
Charley Bates arrives and attacks the murderer, calling for the others to help him. The search party and an angry mob arrive demand-
ing justice. Sikes climbs onto the roof with a rope, intending to
lower himself to escape in the midst of the confusion. However, he
loses his balance when he imagines that he sees Nancy's eyes before
him. The rope catches around his neck, and he falls to his death with
his head in an accidental noose.

Summary: Chapter 51

Oliver and his friends travel to the town of his birth, with Monks in
tow, to meet Mr. Grimwig. There, Monks reveals that he and his
mother found a letter and a will after his father's death, both of
which they destroyed. The letter was addressed to Agnes Fleming's
mother, and it contained a confession from Leeford about their
affair. The will stated that, if his illegitimate child were a girl, she
should inherit the estate unconditionally. If it were a boy, he would
inherit the estate only if he committed no illegal or guilty act. Otherwise, Monks and his mother would receive the fortune. Upon
learning of his daughter's shameful involvement with a married
man, Agnes's father fled his hometown and changed his family's
name. Agnes ran away to save her family the shame of her condition, and her father died soon thereafter of a broken heart. His other
small daughter was taken in by a poor couple who died soon after.
Mrs. Maylie took pity on the little girl and raised her as her niece.
That child is Rose. Mr. Bumble and Mrs. Bumble confess to their
part in concealing Oliver's history, and Mr. Brownlow ensures that

they never hold public office again. Harry has given up his political ambitions and vowed to live as a poor clergyman. Knowing that she no longer stands in the way of Harry's ambitions, Rose agrees to marry him.

SUMMARY: CHAPTER 52

Fagin is sentenced to death for his many crimes. On his miserable last night alive, Brownlow and Oliver visit him in his jail cell to find out the location of papers verifying Oliver's identity, which Monks had entrusted to Fagin.

SUMMARY: CHAPTER 53

> [W]ithout strong affection and humanity of heart, and
> gratitude to that Being whose code is Mercy and
> whose great attribute is Benevolence . . . happiness
> can never be attained.   (See QUOTATIONS, p. 66)

Noah is pardoned because he testifies against Fagin. Charley turns to an honest life and becomes a successful grazier, a person who feeds cattle before they are taken to market. Brownlow arranges for Monks's property to be divided between Monks and Oliver. Monks travels to the New World, where he squanders his share of the inheritance and lives a sordid life that lands him in prison, where he dies. Brownlow adopts Oliver as his son. He, Losberne, and Grimwig take up residence near the rural church over which Harry presides.

ANALYSIS CHAPTERS 49–53

The long story surrounding Mr. Leeford's marriage is told to demonstrate the disastrous consequences of economically motivated marriages. Dickens's romanticism manifests itself in the difference between Oliver and his half-brother. Oliver, the child of Leeford's love affair, is virtuous and innocent. Monks, the result of an economic marriage, is morally twisted by his obsession with wealth. This obsession with money leads him down a long, dark path of nefarious crimes and conspiracies.

Throughout *Oliver Twist*, Dickens criticizes the Victorian stereotype of the poor as criminals from birth. However, after a strident critique of the representation of the poor as hereditary criminals, he portrays Monks as a criminal whose nature has been determined since birth. Brownlow tells Monks, "You . . . from your cradle were gall and bitterness to your own father's heart, and . . . all evil passions, vice, and profligacy, festered [in you]." Monks's evil character seems less the product of his own decisions than of his birth.

Oliver Twist is full of mistaken, assumed, and changed identities. Oliver joins his final domestic scene by assuming yet another identity. Once the mystery of his real identity is revealed, he quickly exchanges it for another, becoming Brownlow's adopted son. After all the fuss and the labyrinthine conspiracies to conceal Oliver's identity, it is ironic that he gives it up almost as soon as he discovers it.

The final chapters quickly deliver the justice that has been delayed throughout the novel. Fagin dies on the gallows. Sikes hangs himself by accident—it is as though the hand of fate or a higher authority reaches out to execute him. Mr. and Mrs. Bumble are deprived of the right to ever hold public office again. They descend into poverty and suffer the same privations they had forced on paupers in the past. Monks never reforms, nor does life show him any mercy. True to Brownlow's characterization of him as bad from birth, he continues his idle, evil ways and dies in an American prison. For him, there is no redemption. Like Noah, he serves as a foil—a character whose attributes contrast with, and thereby accentuate, those of another—to Oliver's character. He is as evil, twisted, and mean while Oliver is good, virtuous, and kind. Oliver and all of his friends, of course, enjoy a blissful, fairy-tale ending. Everyone takes up residence in the same neighborhood and lives together like one big, happy family.

Perhaps the strangest part of the concluding section of *Oliver Twist* is Leeford's condition for Oliver's inheritance. Leeford states in his will that, if his child were a son, he would inherit his estate "only on the stipulation that in his minority he should never have stained his name with any public act of dishonor, meanness, cowardice, or wrong." It seems strange that a father would consign his child to lifelong poverty as well as the stigma of illegitimacy if the son ever committed a single wrong in childhood. In the same way that the court is willing to punish Oliver for crimes committed by another, Leeford is ready to punish Oliver for any small misdeed merely because he hated his first son, Monks, so much.

One contradiction that critics of *Oliver Twist* have pointed out is that although Dickens spends much of the novel openly attacking retributive justice, the conclusion of the novel is quick to deliver such justice. At the story's end, crimes are punished harshly, and devilish characters are still hereditary devils to the very end.

The only real change is that Oliver is now acknowledged as a hereditary angel rather than a hereditary devil. No one, it seems, can escape the identity dealt to him or her at birth. The real crime of characters like Mr. Bumble and Fagin may not have been mistreating a defenseless child—it may have been mistreating a child who was born for a better life.

Yet Dickens's crusade for forgiveness and tolerance is upheld by his treatment of more minor characters, like Nancy, whose memory is sanctified, and Charley Bates, who redeems himself and enters honest society. These characters' fates demonstrate that the individual can indeed rise above his or her circumstances, and that an unfortunate birth does not have to guarantee an unfortunate life and legacy.

SUMMARY & ANALYSIS

IMPORTANT QUOTATIONS EXPLAINED

1. So they established the rule that all poor people should have the alternative (for they would compel nobody, not they) of being starved by a gradual process in the house, or by a quick one out of it. With this view, they contracted with the waterworks to lay on an unlimited supply of water, and with a corn-factor to supply periodically small quantities of oatmeal, and issued three meals of thin gruel a day, with an onion twice a week and half a roll on Sundays. They made a great many other wise and humane regulations . . . kindly undertook to divorce poor married people . . . instead of compelling a man to support his family, as they had theretofore done, took his family away from him, and made him a bachelor! There is no saying how many applicants for relief, under these last two heads, might have started up in all classes of society, if it had not been coupled with the workhouse; but the board were long-headed men, and had provided for this difficulty. The relief was inseparable from the workhouse and the gruel, and that frightened people.

This passage, from Chapter 2, describes the conditions in the workhouse to which the orphan Oliver has just been sent. The function of this description is twofold: first, to provoke our sympathies for young Oliver and his fellow unfortunates, and second, to register Dickens's protest against the welfare policy and practice of charity in the England of his time. Three years before the publication of *Oliver Twist,* the British Parliament passed a controversial amendment to the nation's "poor-laws." This amendment stipulated that the poor could receive public assistance only if they took up residence in official workhouses and abided by their regulations. In these workhouses, husbands were separated from wives, and living conditions were often abysmal. Lurking behind the establishment of workhouses were the assumptions that moral virtue lay in work, that work led necessarily to success, that economic failure was the result of laziness, and that, therefore, poverty was a sign of moral degeneracy. In Dickens's opinion, charity based on this kind of premise did far more harm than good to the material and moral situations of its recipients. In this passage, and throughout the early chapters of the novel, he adopts a sarcastic, harshly satirical tone to make this point. Dickens, in fact, says the exact opposite of what he really means and does no more than state the truth. All of the conditions he describes did actually exist. Rather than exaggerating to make his point, Dickens relies on the inherent absurdity of the way English society treated the poor to manifest itself through his description.

2. Who can describe the pleasure and delight, the peace
    of mind and soft tranquility, the sickly boy felt in the
    balmy air and among the green hills and rich woods of
    an inland village! Who can tell how scenes of peace
    and quietude sink into the minds of pain-worn
    dwellers in close and noisy places, and carry their own
    freshness deep into their jaded hearts! Men who have
    lived in crowded, pent-up streets, through lives of toil,
    and who have never wished for change—men to
    whom custom has indeed been second nature, and
    who have come almost to love each brick and stone
    that formed the narrow boundaries of their daily
    walks—even they, with the hand of death upon them,
    have been known to yearn at last for one short
    glimpse of Nature's face, and, carried far from the
    scenes of their old pains and pleasures, have seemed to
    pass at once into a new state of being.

In Dickens's time, England was rapidly becoming an industrial,
urban society. Dickens's works are overwhelmingly concerned with
the social and psychological conditions that city life fostered, and he
is known as one of the first great urban European authors. Yet, in
this passage from Chapter 32, describing Oliver's sojourn to the
countryside with Mrs. Maylie and Rose, the author reveals his pro-
found skepticism about the influence of urban life on the human
character. This passage praises the purity and health of the rural
environment and claims outright that even a lifelong city-dweller
has in his blood a faint longing for the "new state of being" to which
nature can elevate him. Dickens goes on to note that, in the country,
even "the poor people" are "neat and clean." The squalor and starvation that characterize urban poverty are not present in rural
England. Given the eagerness of England's rural poor to migrate to
the city, it seems unlikely that this assessment is realistic. In many
ways, Dickens's idealized vision marks him all the more clearly as an
urban writer, since his gritty portraits of city life are based on real
experience, while his blissful portrait of rural life seems more the
product of wistful fantasy.

3. "Stay another moment," interposed Rose. . . . "Will you return to this gang of robbers, and to this man, when a word can save you? What fascination is it that can take you back, and make you cling to wickedness and misery?" "When ladies as young, and good, and beautiful as you are," replied the girl [Nancy] steadily, "give away your hearts, love will carry you all lengths—even such as you, who have home, friends, other admirers, everything, to fill them. When such as I, who have no certain roof but the coffin-lid, and no friend in sickness or death but the hospital nurse, set our rotten hearts on any man, and let him fill the place that has been a blank through all our wretched lives, who can hope to cure us? Pity us, lady—pity us for having only one feeling of the woman left and for having that turned, by a heavy judgment, from a comfort and a pride into a new means of violence and suffering."

This exchange takes place between Rose and Nancy in Chapter 40. It is one of the most emotionally heightened conversations in the novel, and it represents a sophisticated treatment of the moral and social issues that dominate the story. Nancy, a prostitute, embodies for Dickens all the degradation into which poverty can force otherwise good people. Rose, on the other hand, represents all the purity that comes from good breeding. Both women embody the feminine compassion that compels them to help Oliver. That feminine compassion, maternal and sisterly when directed toward Oliver, is also what binds Nancy to her vice-ridden lover Sikes. In this passage, Dickens emphasizes the key role that environment plays in distinguishing vice from virtue: the same loyalty to a loved one that would be a virtue in Rose is a self-destructive force for Nancy. Though Nancy is compassionate and intelligent, she deflects Rose's attempts to save her from her life of crime, thus proving that the damage done by a bad upbringing is irrevocable. Yet Nancy's decision to return to a life of "vice" is arguably the most noble—if foolhardy—act in the entire novel. Her love for Sikes and her compassion for Oliver together compel her to sacrifice her own life. Though Dickens clearly approves of the second emotion far more than the first, it is likely that they stem from the same impulse in Nancy's character.

4.   At times he [Sikes] turned with desperate determination, resolved to beat this phantom off, though it should look him dead; but the hair rose on his head and his blood stood still, for it had turned with him and was behind him then. He had kept it before him that morning, but it was behind now— always. He leaned his back against a bank, and felt that it stood above him, visibly out against the cold night sky. He threw himself upon the road—on his back upon the road. At his head it stood, silent, erect, and still—a living grave-stone, with its epitaph in blood. Let no man talk of murderers escaping justice, and hint that Providence must sleep. There were twenty score of violent deaths in one long minute of that agony of fear.

After murdering Nancy, Sikes flees London, only to find that his conscience will not let him escape. This passage, from Chapter 48, embodies an idea that has fascinated many great authors—the idea that a guilty conscience is its own punishment, worse than any that the law can assign. The entire account of Sikes's flight is also among the most psychologically sophisticated passages in the novel. Up until this point, Sikes has been a pure villain. In his guilt, however, he becomes more realistically human. We probably cannot sympathize with Sikes, but, in this chapter, we do see the world through his wretched eyes. Moreover, Dickens's vivid descriptions allow us to experience Sikes's sensation of being hunted, by both external and more horrifying internal pursuers.

5. I have said that they were truly happy; and without strong affection and humanity of heart, and gratitude to that Being whose code is Mercy and whose great attribute is Benevolence to all things that breathe, happiness can never be attained. Within the altar of the old village church there stands a white marble tablet which bears as yet but one word: "Agnes". . . . I believe that the shade of Agnes sometimes hovers round the solemn nook. I believe it none the less because that nook is in a Church, and she was weak and erring.

The final passage of the novel sums up Dickens's moral and religious vision. On the one hand, Dickens considers a firm and true belief in God to be an essential prerequisite of both moral rectitude and earthly happiness. On the other hand, the novel has not been kind to characters such as Mr. Bumble, who prattle on about Christian values, but whose behavior is notably lacking in "Benevolence" and who are quick to condemn others as sinners. The description of Agnes's grave is an attack on puritanical religion, which would consider adultery to be an unforgivable sin. The novel's faith in Christian values is as wholehearted as its attacks on Christian hypocrisy are biting.

KEY FACTS

FULL TITLE
  Oliver Twist: The Parish Boy's Progress

AUTHOR
  Charles Dickens

TYPE OF WORK
  Novel

GENRE
  Children's story; detective story; novel of social protest

LANGUAGE
  English

TIME AND PLACE WRITTEN
  1837–38, London

DATE OF FIRST PUBLICATION
  Published in serial form between February 1837 and April
  1839; first book edition published in November 1838

PUBLISHER
  First published serially in *Bentley's Miscellany,* a periodical
  edited by Dickens

NARRATOR
  Anonymous narrator

POINT OF VIEW
  The narrator is third person omniscient, and assumes the points
  of view of various characters in turn. The narrator's tone is not
  objective; it is sympathetic to the protagonists and far less so to
  the novel's other characters. When dealing with hypocritical or
  morally objectionable characters, the narrative voice is often
  ironic or sarcastic.

TONE
  Sentimental, sometimes ironic, hyperbolic, crusading

TENSE
  Past

SETTING (TIME)
1830s

SETTING (PLACE)
London and environs; an unnamed smaller English city; the English countryside

PROTAGONIST
Oliver Twist

MAJOR CONFLICT
Although Oliver is fundamentally righteous, the social environment in which he is raised encourages thievery and prostitution. Oliver struggles to find his identity and rise above the abject conditions of the lower class.

RISING ACTION
Oliver is taken care of by a gang of London thieves, but refuses to participate in their thievery. An upper-class family takes him in, but the thieves and a mysterious character, Monks, continue to pursue him.

CLIMAX
Nancy is murdered for disclosing Monks's plans to Oliver's guardians. Mr. Brownlow gets the full story of Oliver's origins from Monks.

FALLING ACTION
Fagin is executed and Sikes dies; Oliver and his new family live out their days in happiness.

THEMES
The failures of charity; the folly of individualism; purity in a corrupt city; the countryside idealized

MOTIFS
Disguised or mistaken identities; hidden family relationships; surrogate families; Oliver's face

SYMBOLS
Characters' names; Bull's-eye; London Bridge

FORESHADOWING
The truth about Oliver's parentage is foreshadowed by the portrait in Mr. Brownlow's house, by the locket that Old Sally has stolen, and by Monks's pursuit of Oliver.

KEY FACTS

STUDY QUESTIONS & ESSAY TOPICS

STUDY QUESTIONS

1. *Victorian stereotypes about the poor asserted that poverty and vice were fundamentally connected and that, moreover, both were hereditary traits: the poor were supposedly bad from birth. How does Dickens approach such stereotypes?*

On the surface, Dickens appears to be using *Oliver Twist* to criticize the Victorian idea that the poor were naturally destined for lives of degradation and desperation. Dickens satirizes characters who voice such an opinion, such as Mr. Bumble, Mr. Grimwig, and Mrs. Sowerberry. The latter, for instance, declares that children like Oliver "are born to be murderers and robbers from their very cradle." In addition, characters like Nancy, Charley Bates, and Oliver stand in direct opposition to the assertion that an individual who happens to be poor is also born without any innate sense of right and wrong. However, on a more subtle level, Oliver may be interpreted as a character who lends support to the very stereotypes Dickens seems to be condemning. At the end of the novel, we discover that Oliver is, in fact, the child of well-off parents, and a Victorian reader could interpret the novel as saying that Oliver's seemingly innate goodness is inherited from them. Moreover, with a few obvious exceptions, most of the poor characters depicted are morally reprehensible, or at the very least somewhat laughable as people. Finally, while the character of Monks explicitly violates the connection of vice with poverty, he represents some support for the argument that moral shortcomings are the product of nature, not nurture. Brownlow tells Monks that, "You . . . from your cradle were gall and bitterness to your own father's heart, and . . . all evil passions, vice, and profligacy, festered [in you]." It seems, then, that vice and virtue may be hereditary traits, present in an individual "from [the] cradle."

2.   *Consider the female characters of Nancy, Rose Maylie,
      and Agnes Fleming. How are the three women different?
      How are they similar? What do their differences and
      similarities suggest about Dickens's ideas about women?*

The differences between the three women are explicitly stated in the
novel. Rose is a young lady of good breeding and perfect chastity.
Nancy, in contrast, is a girl raised on the street and a prostitute.
Agnes, as a young girl of good breeding who nonetheless committed
a fatal sexual indiscretion in her affair with Mr. Leeford, stands
somewhere in between Rose, a model of purity, and Nancy, a model
of sin. Each woman's social standing is closely bound to her sexual
history. Less obvious are the similarities between them, which center
around the sacrifices each makes for others. Nancy sacrifices her life
for the sake of Oliver, a boy she barely knows. Agnes gives her life to
save her family from her own ill repute. On a lesser scale, even Rose
makes a great sacrifice when she refuses to marry Harry Maylie, fear-
ing that her dubious birth will harm his chances for career advancement. Dickens passes overwhelmingly favorable judgments on each
of these women. In doing so, he demonstrates a broad-minded will-
ingness to forgive the sexual indiscretions of which two of them are
guilty. Yet he also displays a thoroughly Victorian fondness for
humility and self-sacrifice in women. The ideal woman, it would
seem, must be prepared, and even glad, to live and die for others.
    Again and again in Dickens's novels, female characters appear
who, like Nancy and Agnes, commit sexual indiscretions at some
point in their lives, but who in one way or another redeem themselves, displaying generosity and love as well as repentance. It is
interesting to note that while Dickens goes to great lengths to establish that these fallen women are still human beings worthy of forgiveness and redemption, every one of them either dies or is
transported by the end of the novel in which she appears. As with
Nancy, many of these female characters are offered the chance to
reject their pasts and start over, but this new beginning is never to
be. It is as if Dickens advocates in principle the idea that sexually
tainted women could be reconciled with respectable English society,
but he cannot actually bring himself to imagine a scenario in which
this social rebirth actually happens.

3. *Discuss the portrait of the criminal justice system presented in* Oliver Twist.

We might hope that legal justice in *Oliver Twist* would be blind, not taking into account people's social status, gender, or age. Unfortunately, however, in early nineteenth-century England, such factors did seem to matter. The legal system portrayed in *Oliver Twist*, however, is heavily biased in favor of middle-class and upper-class individuals. Oliver enters courtrooms twice in the novel. The magistrate who presides over Gamfield's petition to take Oliver on as an apprentice is half blind. Only by chance does he see the terror on Oliver's face and so decide to save him from life as a chimney sweep. With reference to this trial, the phrase "justice is blind" seems ironic. Like the magistrate, the justice system is half blind. It is generally unable to perceive the perspective or interest of the poor. Oliver's trial for stealing a handkerchief also highlights the precarious position of the poor in the eyes of the law. Mr. Fang is the presiding magistrate at Oliver's trial, and the law has fangs ready to harshly punish any unfortunate pauper brought to face justice. Without hard evidence, without witnesses, and despite the protests of the victim of the crime, Mr. Fang convicts Oliver. Mr. Fang is biased against Oliver from the moment he steps into the courtroom. He does not view Oliver as an individual but as a representative of the criminal poor. Again, the phrase "justice is blind" can be applied ironically to *Oliver Twist*. The magistrate is blinded by his society's stereotypes about the poor. The novel's portrait of legal justice will change considerably by the end, when it condemns Fagin, guarantees Oliver his inheritance, and generally helps ensure fair outcomes in the characters' lives. This change occurs when Oliver receives the backing of wealthy individuals like Brownlow and the Maylies. Once Oliver gains wealth and social status, the law seemingly regains its sight.

SUGGESTED ESSAY TOPICS

1. In Chapters 48 and 52, Dickens explores the consequences of Sikes's and Fagin's crimes. Is the narrative technique in these chapters different from that in the rest of the novel? If so, how? How does the reader's perspective on Sikes and Fagin change in these chapters? How do these chapters address the issues of guilt and punishment?

2. Discuss the character of Fagin. To what extent does anti-Semitism influence Dickens's portrait of him? Should Fagin be taken to represent all Jews? May he be taken to represent anything else?

3. *Oliver Twist* is full of thievery. Some of it is committed by criminals like Sikes against respectable people like the Maylies, while some of it is committed by "respectable" people like Mrs. Mann and Mr. Bumble against the poor. How are these two types of thievery different? What do they have in common? Also, consider the various ways in which other people "rob" Oliver of his identity. What does the prevalence of thievery in the novel say about the world that it portrays?

4. What role does clothing play in the various characters' identities? Consider Nancy's disguise, the new suit that Brownlow purchases for Oliver, and Mr. Bumble's regret at giving up the office of parish beadle.

5. How does Dickens represent marriage in *Oliver Twist*? Compare and contrast the marriages of Mr. Bumble and Mrs. Corney, of Rose and Harry, and of Mr. Leeford and Monks's mother. Consider also the prevalence of "families" that do not center around a marriage: for example, Oliver, Brownlow, Grimwig, and Mrs. Bedwin; or Mrs. Maylie, Rose, and Mr. Losberne.

Review & Resources

Quiz

1. Who runs the home for young orphans where Oliver lives for nine years?

   A. Mr. Bumble
   B. Mrs. Mann
   C. Agnes Fleming
   D. Miss Hannigan

2. How does Oliver violate the rules of the workhouse?

   A. By asking for more gruel
   B. By taking the Lord's name in vain
   C. By running a pickpocketing ring
   D. By spreading revolutionary ideology among the paupers

3. What is Mr. Gamfield's profession?

   A. Undertaker
   B. Chef
   C. Butler
   D. Chimney sweep

4. What is Mr. Sowerberry's profession?

   A. Undertaker
   B. Chef
   C. Butler
   D. Chimney sweep

5. How does Noah Claypole incur Oliver's wrath?

   A. By insulting his mother
   B. By insulting his clothes
   C. By mistreating Charlotte
   D. By stealing food from the larder

6. What is Jack Dawkins's nickname?

    A. Toby Crackit
    B. The Artful Dodger
    C. Loopy
    D. The Jackal

7. Of what ethnicity is Fagin?

    A. Irish
    B. Italian
    C. Mixed race
    D. Jewish

8. Mr. Brownlow notices that Oliver bears a close resemblance to whom?

    A. Mrs. Bedwin
    B. The woman in the portrait on his wall
    C. Queen Victoria
    D. The Christ child

9. What does Nancy pretend to be in order to drag Oliver back to Fagin?

    A. A truant officer
    B. Oliver's sister
    C. A workhouse official
    D. Oliver's mother

10. Who comes to Oliver's defense after Fagin recaptures him?

    A. Jack Dawkins
    B. Charley Bates
    C. Nancy
    D. Mr. Brownlow

11. Who is shot in the attempted burglary of the Maylie house?

    A. Oliver
    B. Bill Sikes
    C. Bull's-eye
    D. Toby Crackit

12. Which character falls deathly ill in the countryside?

    A.   Oliver
    B.   Mrs. Maylie
    C.   Mr. Bumble
    D.   Rose Maylie

13. Why does Mr. Bumble propose to Mrs. Corney?

    A.   He wants to take revenge on Oliver
    B.   She reminds him of his late wife
    C.   He wants children
    D.   He wants her money

14. What did Old Sally steal from Agnes Fleming?

    A.   A will
    B.   A marriage certificate
    C.   An engraved watch
    D.   A gold locket

15. Why does Rose refuse to marry Harry Maylie?

    A.   Because they are related
    B.   Because she does not want to stand in the way of his ambition
    C.   Because she wants to marry someone who would be a better provider
    D.   Because she is in love with Bill Sikes

16. To whom does the dog Bull's-eye belong?

    A.   Bill Sikes
    B.   Oliver
    C.   Monks
    D.   Mr. Brownlow

17. What is Nancy's profession?

    A.   Flower-seller
    B.   Nurse
    C.   Prostitute
    D.   Con artist

18. Where does Nancy meet Rose and Brownlow?

    A.   London Bridge
    B.   The Three Cripples
    C.   The Old Victoria Theater
    D.   A blacking factory

19. What image haunts Bill Sikes after he commits murder?

    A.   Oliver's face
    B.   A bloody club
    C.   The gallows
    D.   Nancy's eyes

20. Which three characters are all related to Oliver?

    A.   Harry Maylie, Mrs. Maylie, Rose Maylie
    B.   Rose Maylie, Monks, Agnes Fleming
    C.   Agnes Fleming, Old Sally, Mr. Losberne
    D.   Monks, Bill Sikes, Agnes Fleming

21. Where does Oliver last see Fagin?

    A.   In a courtroom
    B.   In the West Indies
    C.   Underneath London Bridge
    D.   In a jail cell

22. Which character's real name is Edward Leeford?

    A.   Jack Dawkins
    B.   Monks
    C.   Oliver
    D.   Noah Claypole

23. Which character is subject to violent spasmodic fits?

    A.   Monks
    B.   Fagin
    C.   Bull's-eye
    D.   Mr. Grimwig

24. Which of the following novels did Dickens *not* write?

    A. *Bleak House*
    B. *The Mill on the Floss*
    C. *The Pickwick Papers*
    D. *Great Expectations*

25. Dickens wrote *Oliver Twist* in response to what piece of legislation?

    A. The Law of Estates and Inheritance
    B. The Poor Law of 1834
    C. The institution of the death penalty
    D. The Decency Act

SUGGESTIONS FOR FURTHER READING

BAYLEY, JOHN. *"Oliver Twist*: 'Things as They Really Are.'" In John Gross and Gabriel Pearson, ed. *Dickens and the Twentieth Century.* London: Routledge, 1962.

COLLINS, PHILIP. *Dickens and Crime.* London: Macmillan, 1968.

DUNN, RICHARD J. OLIVER TWIST: *Whole Heart and Soul.* New York: Twayne Publishers, 1993.

MILLER, J. HILLIS. *Charles Dickens: The World of His Novels.* Cambridge, Massachusetts: Harvard University Press, 1958.

RAINA, BADRI. *Dickens and the Dialectic of Growth.* Madison, Wisconsin: University of Wisconsin Press, 1986.

SLATER, MICHAEL. *Dickens and Women.* Stanford, California: Stanford University Press, 1983.

SWISHER, CLARICE, ed. *Readings on Charles Dickens.* San Diego: Greenhaven Press, 1998.

A Note on the Type

The typeface used in SparkNotes study guides is Sabon, created by master typographer Jan Tschichold in 1964. Tschichold revolutionized the field of graphic design twice: first with his use of asymmetrical layouts and sanserif type in the 1930s when he was affiliated with the Bauhaus, then by abandoning assymetry and calling for a return to the classic ideals of design. Sabon, his only extant typeface, is emblematic of his latter program: Tschichold's design is a recreation of the types made by Claude Garamond, the great French typographer of the Renaissance, and his contemporary Robert Granjon. Fittingly, it is named for Garamond's apprentice, Jacques Sabon.

SPARKNOTES
TEST PREPARATION
GUIDES

The SparkNotes team figured it was time to cut standardized tests down to size. We've studied the tests for you, so that SparkNotes test prep guides are:

Smarter:
Packed with critical-thinking skills and test-taking strategies that will improve your score.

Better:
Fully up to date, covering all new features of the tests, with study tips on every type of question.

Faster:
Our books cover exactly what you need to know for the test. No more, no less.

SparkNotes Study Guides: